HOLY WEEK FOR TEENS

Meena Awad

HOLY WEEK FOR TEENS

by

Meena Awad

ST SHENOUDA MONASTERY
SYDNEY, AUSTRALIA
2014

HOLY WEEK FOR TEENS

ST SHENOUDA MONASTERY
8419 Putty Rd,
Putty, NSW, Australia

www.stshenoudamonastery.org.au

ISBN 13: 978-0-9873400-7-8

About the Author

Meena Awad is a member of Archangel Michael and St Bishoy Coptic Orthodox Church in Sydney, Australia. He is extensively involved in theological education and service for High School and University youth.

Cover Design:

Mariana Hanna
In and Out Creation Pty Ltd
inandoutcreations.com.au

Text Layout:

Hani Ghaly,
Begoury Graphics
begourygraphics@gmail.com

CONTENTS

INTRODUCTION

Teens Guide for Holy Week highlights the most crucial and important events of Holy Week. It is a simple yet detailed description of the day-by-day and night-by-night events that took place during the final week of Christ's life, giving relevant contemplations and practical applications that suits teenagers. The book contains sayings of the Fathers and what their thoughts are on certain events that took place during the Passion of Christ. Within are also small reflections which aim to help you meditate on the current happenings in your own life or to further reflect on the meaning behind certain words or events.

This guide is aimed at teenagers, youth and all who want to benefit from the Holy Week.

LAZARUS SATURDAY

Events

LAZARUS SATURDAY

The gospel of St John tells us the story of Christ raising His friend Lazarus from the dead. The story goes that a messenger was sent to Jesus saying "Lord, behold, he (Lazarus) whom you love is sick." In turn, Jesus sent the messenger back with comforting words. But instead of journeying to Bethany, the place where Lazarus was, He lingered in the town He was in for two more days then travelled to Judea where He told His disciples that Lazarus had died.

This surprised the disciples as they knew that Christ was more than capable of healing Lazarus and Bethany was not too far from where they were. Jesus could very easily have gone over on a quick detour, healed Lazarus (who most certainly was a dear friend of Christ's), then continued His objective. Little did they know the entire saga was all part of His great plan. Jesus said, "Lazarus is dead. And I am glad for your sakes that I was not there that you may believe. Nevertheless, let us go to him."

Jesus then arrives in Bethany and finds that Lazarus has been dead and buried four days. There was an old Jewish thought that the soul of the departed would linger around its dead body for three days, but on the fourth day it would depart. Bringing Lazarus to life thus seemed an impossible task. As Jesus approached, Martha ran to Him and a fascinating conversation took place.

Martha: "Lord, if you had been here, my brother would not have died. But even now I know that whatever You ask of God, God will give You."

Jesus: "Your brother will rise again."

Martha: "I know that he will rise again in the resurrection at the last day."

Jesus: "I am the resurrection and the life. He who believes in Me, though he may die, he shall live. And whoever lives and believes in Me shall never die. Do you believe this?"

Martha: "Yes, Lord I believe that You are the Christ, the Son of God, who is to come into the world."

As mentioned above, this conversation is very intriguing. Allow me to take you into the depth of what is being said. Martha clearly had great faith; in her initial statement she honestly believed that Jesus could have healed Lazarus if He had arrived whilst Lazarus was alive. Yet this statement is rather bitter sweet. While it shows the faith that Martha possessed, it also indicates that Martha still does not fully understand who Jesus is. When she says, "Whatever You ask of God, God will give You," Martha proves that she does not understand that Jesus is God! As God, He has full divine authority to act as He wills.

Jesus then replies with what proves to be a major theme across His life, ministry, death and resurrection: "I am the resurrection and the life." Jesus lovingly corrects Martha and in this one statement not only explains to her that He has power to raise the dead both in the last day and now, but also empowers Martha to believe that He is God!

> **What the Fathers Say**
>
> *"He is stoned, but is not taken. He prays, but He hears prayer. He weeps, but He causes tears to cease. He asks where Lazarus was laid, for He was Man; but He raises Lazarus, for He was God."*
>
> – St Gregory of Nazianzen

Soon after, Martha's sister Mary comes and they all head toward the tomb where Lazarus was buried. As they reach the tomb, Jesus begins to weep and is deeply sorrowful. He then instructs onlookers to remove the stone, the door of the tomb. At this request, and at the sight of Jesus weeping it seems that Martha reverts back to her earlier misunderstanding and she says, "Lord, by this time there is a stench, for he has been dead four days." Jesus quickly corrects and reminds her, "Did I not say to you that if you would believe you would see the glory of God?" This question goes out to all of us. Jesus has made very clear to us that He really is God. Yet how often do we remain unbelieving, even if we have just told Him we trust Him?

People, Places and Things

Lazarus

Lazarus was a personal friend of Jesus. He was the brother of Mary and Martha. Lazarus was raised by Jesus after being dead four days. Lazarus was present at the Passover in Bethany six days later, and given his celebrity status and that Jesus brought him back to life after death which was living proof of the Divinity of Jesus, the chief priests wanted to kill him. Lazarus means "One whom God helps" and is the shortened form of the popular Old Testament name Eleazer. Tradition tells us that after Pentecost, the Apostles ordained Lazarus to be the bishop of Cyprus. Forty years after this, he departed.

Jesus then looks up to Heaven and prays, crying out, "Lazarus, come forth!" At these words, Lazarus, "he who had died," came out alive and well and Jesus was truly glorified with this incredible evidence of His Divinity.

This entire episode is very clear evidence of the true nature of Jesus Christ as full Man and full God. Full Man in that He weeps and is sorrowful; emotions felt by a mortal. At the same time, the raising of Lazarus from the dead by His own authority highlights Jesus' divinity and shows He is full God.

The importance of Lazarus Saturday is often under written. But in fact, it was due to the

Salome

Salome is the mother of the apostles James and John. She is the one who asked Jesus to allow her sons to sit at His right and left in the Kingdom of Heaven. She is also the wife of Zebedee. Some say that she was the sister of Mary the mother of God, making James and John the Lord's cousins. Others believe that she was Jesus's midwife, and delivered Him from Mary's womb.

Mary Magdalene

Mary Magdalene was from a Galilean town called Magdala. Given its location from Nazareth, there is a chance that Jesus and His earthly guardian father Joseph may have practised their trade of carpentry in Magdala. Many say that Mary Magdalene was a prostitute, but this is not known for sure. All that is biblically confirmed is that Mary Magdalene was possessed by seven demons. The Lord cleansed her and exorcized the demons out of her, and she became a devout follower of Jesus ever since. She is notably the first witness of the Lord's resurrection. She was also a brave preacher of Christianity after she had received the Holy Spirit on the day of Pentecost.

events of this day that the leaders of the Jewish nation became determined to kill Jesus. Over the three years of the Lord's ministry, people in the thousands followed Him, not only believing Him to be a great teacher but also the long awaited Messiah.

What the Fathers Say

"If you were to ask: 'Why did the Evangelist state clearly here that the Lord loved Lazarus?' Our response would be: 'So that we may not be disappointed nor abandon the Lord when good men, who are steadfast in virtue and loved by God, get sick' "

– St John Chrysostom.

Jesus turned many to Him with His incredible yet tender words, His unprecedented physical presence and His unconditionally loving nature. But what made many believe that Jesus was unquestionably the Messiah was His ability to do amazing miracles and none was more amazing than the raising of Lazarus from the dead. Jesus Himself said, "Believe Me that I am in the Father and the Father in Me, or else believe Me for the sake of the works themselves." If you didn't believe Jesus was the Messiah before He raised Lazarus from the dead, then you sure did after!

Thus, those who opposed Jesus felt this to be the last straw; they now had to kill Him and by whatever means necessary.

Lazarus Saturday acts as a bridge between the great lent and passion week. Traditionally the church used to fast the great lent directly after the feast of Epiphany (the baptism of Jesus), as is mentioned in the gospel of St Matthew 3:16 – 4:1. And Lazarus Saturday was always the day before Palm Sunday, as it was the last biblically noted thing He did before His triumphal entry into Jerusalem. However, during the papacy of Pope Demetrius the 1st, 12th Patriarch of the See of Alexandria, it was decided, amongst other reasons, that certain preparation was needed before entering into Holy Week. Thus, the great lent was moved and joined to Holy Week beginning at Lazarus Saturday.

Liturgically, Lazarus Saturday is neither a part of Holy Week or lent but is awkwardly centered in between both seasons. The liturgical tune is neither in the repentant great lent tune, nor is it in the Joyful Palm Sunday tune or in the sad Holy Week tune, but in fact is in the normal annual tune.

The aim of the service is to not only remind us of the incredible "Nature of the incarnate Logos" who is full man and full God, but it is also to wake us up from our spiritual death, hence certain responses as, "Hail to Lazarus whom He raised after four days; oh my Lord Jesus, raise my heart that was killed by the evil one".

Reflections

Imagine you are Lazarus who rose from the dead and had a new lease on life, what would you change?

PALM SUNDAY EVE

Events

PALM SUNDAY EVE

On this evening, the Church recounts one of the most inspirational stories of honouring Jesus ever told.

After Jesus raised Lazarus from the dead, Jesus and His disciples returned to Bethany and Jesus had supper at the house of Lazarus, Martha and Mary. The Lord sat with Lazarus at the table while Martha was serving them all. While this took place, Mary, the sister of Lazarus, stumbled in and fell to the floor in reverence, worshiping Him. As she did this, she opened a flask containing a pound of "very costly oil of spikenard." As she poured the precious oil onto the precious feet of God, she began to wipe the Lord's feet with her hair.

In Jewish tradition, the hair of a woman was her pride. The reason women are told to cover their heads in church is to show humility before God, covering their glory as the Cherubim and Seraphim do whilst in the presence of God. So for Mary to wipe the Lord's feet with her hair was to totally humble herself before God.

This must have been such a spectacular site. To see a family member or a friend, totally humbling himself or herself before God has such a contagious effect. St John says that, "the house was filled with the fragrance of the oil." How true this was as the oil used was a powerful substance and surely filled the nostrils of those present with a beautiful scent. Yet more than this beautiful scent is the majestic feeling of reverence and humility that filled the hearts of all those who were witnessing, all except one. In the midst of this great act, Judas

Iscariot, the one who would betray the Messiah, stood up and said aloud, "Why was this oil not sold for three hundred denarii and given to the poor?" Judas was a deceptive and cunning fox. He neither said that as an act of service nor out of love of the poor, but because he took care of the money box and would steal the money that was kept for the poor. The Lord, the Just Judge and discerner of all that is good, turned to Judas and rebuked him and said, "Let her alone; she has kept this for the day of My burial." Turning to all His disciples Jesus said, "For the poor you have with you always, but Me you do not have always."

Notice that Jesus mentions that Mary did this for His burial. Many sermons speak of this on a metaphorical level, but this is also quite literal. When Christ died, He was rushed to the tomb because the next day was the Sabbath and no work was to be done on that day. Those who buried Him hardly had any time to complete a traditional Jewish burial. Thus the anointing by Mary counted as the completion of the Lord's burial four days away from this event.

What the Fathers Say

"Allow sinners to behold Me. For their sakes, I humbled Myself. I will not ascend to heaven, to the place from which I came down, until I bring back the sheep that wandered away from the Father's house. I will lift the sheep on My shoulders and carry them to heaven."

– St Ephraim the Syrian

What the Fathers Say

"Finally, the Lord had also come to Bethany, after having raised Lazarus, in order to follow up the effects of His deed. It is as though He had come to water what He had planted, and to sanctify it so that it would yield adequate fruit."

- Fr Tadros Y Malaty

This event truly is beautiful, for the entire scene appeals to many of our senses. Our eyes behold a loved one bowing down and worshiping God, and our hearts bow down with her. Our noses smell the pure and honest sacrifice made before the Creator of all. Our worshiping knees feel the weight of our bodies, while our spirits ascend with weightlessness to our Abba. Our ears rejoice as they hear the acceptance of this sacrifice from the Saviour's own mouth. Truly what a great act you have done O Mary of Bethany! May we learn to worship and honour our Lord as you have.

The church is decorated in Palm branches for vespers in preparation for the coming of Christ. The reason Palm branches are used is because the gospel writers all speak of the local people cutting down leafy branches from trees and throwing them before the feet of Christ as He triumphantly entered into Jerusalem. The leafy branches that were used by the people were Palm branches, so the Church mimics this action and decorates the church with these same Palm branches.

Liturgical

The hymns and responses are chanted using a special festal and royal tune, the "Hosanna tune". During vespers (and matins the following morning), a procession is performed around the entire church with palms and an icon of the Lord's entry to Jerusalem.

People, Places and Things

Spikenard Oil

Spikenard is an expensive spice that is used as the base ingredient in perfumes. It is a very pure and concentrated oil, and from it numerous other perfumes can be manufactured. Thus, Mary truly offered Jesus her first fruits and gave Him from the purest and best of what she had.

Joanna

Joanna was a disciple of Jesus who followed Him after He healed her from an illness. She helped Jesus a lot in His ministry and would often support Him and the disciples from her own pocket. Her husband's name was Chuza. He was a steward in the house of Herod. Joanna was one of the women who went to anoint the body of Christ on the day of resurrection. Her name means "Yahweh's gift."

Throughout the processions and also during the liturgy, you will hear a special hymn being chanted known as "Evlogimenos" which is translated as, "Blessed is He who comes in the name of the Lord! Hosanna in the Highest" and "Hosanna to the King of Israel." This is exactly what the people sang when they welcomed Jesus into Jerusalem. The hymn calls to mind the prophecies that the Messiah will come from the true lineage of the kings, from the bloodline of David. Thus, we praise the One whom the prophets spoke about, and the One who fulfils all they have prophesied.

The concluding canon (Amen Alleluia) tells us to rejoice for the King is coming! It very briefly recounts the events of Palm Sunday to awaken our minds to the magnitude and significance of the next day.

Reflections

If you were Mary, what would be the most valuable thing in your life that you could offer at Christ's feet?

PALM SUNDAY

Events

PALM SUNDAY

This day marks the Lord's triumphant entrance into Jerusalem. All four Gospels record this incredible event and in celebration of the entry, all four Gospel accounts of the event are read.

Jesus was travelling to Jerusalem from Bethany. On the way He sent two disciples ahead of Him to a local village. He told them they would find a donkey, actually a colt, a baby donkey. He told them to bring it to Him and if anyone asks, "What are you doing with the donkey?" to say, "The Master has need of it." The disciples did so and when the owners asked what they were doing with the donkey, the disciples responded as Jesus instructed and took the donkey to Christ. This is a bit strange. The owner just let them take his donkey. Donkeys aren't cheap. And they definitely aren't just handed out for free. This causes us to believe that the owner of the donkey may have known Jesus and the two disciples who were sent. Some even say that this owner was the father of St Mark or maybe even St Mark himself, but this is just speculation, we don't really know for sure. But it would be pretty cool if it were true!

So, the two disciples bring the donkey to Jesus, throw their clothes on it, and seat Him on the animal. Then an amazing thing takes place. As Jesus is entering into Jerusalem, all the people who had heard of Him came and welcomed Him. A large mass on His left, and a large mass on His right, all waving branches of Palm trees around and throwing their clothes on the floor in front of the colt. All are shouting "Hosanna!" "Hosanna!"

means "save us now." "Hosanna to the Son of David! Blessed is He who comes in the name of the Lord!"

Save us? Save you from what? ... Well to say that Israel had a long history of captivity and national torment is an understatement. Whether it was the Egyptians, the Philistines, the Canaanites, the Assyrians, the Babylonians or the Greeks, the Israelites had it tough. And the period of Christ was no exception. This time, Israel was invaded by the Romans, who imposed both strict taxes and a strict rule of life on the Jewish nation. So the people were crying out for Jesus to save them from the reign of the Roman Empire. Ultimately they wanted an earthly King that would destroy their enemies and set them free from bondage. This is exactly what Jesus did, just not the way the people were expecting it.

If He had just saved them from the Romans, given their history, the Jewish people would have just been captured or plagued by another nation some time further down the track. It would have

What the Fathers Say

"The palm tree branches are symbols of victory. That is why Cicero who had won many trophies was called 'the man of many palm branches'. The Lord overcame the powers of darkness through His death. That is why He was worthy to have bearers of palm branches pave His way."

- Fr Tadros Y Malaty

been a temporary solution to an ongoing problem. So Christ saved them, and us, from the greater slavery. The slavery of sin! And the sting of death! Jesus very well could have saved them from the Romans, it was well in His Power to do so. But He wanted the whole world to be free from sin and joined to Him eternally, knowing perfectly well that the good news of this salvation would provide enough joy to get through any captivity by any earthly being, rather than a small amount of people being free from invasion for only a small period of time. Jesus's mission was much bigger than what the people understood. It is however really sad to see that many of the people who were crying out "Hosanna" cry out "Crucify Him" only five days later....

The Lord's triumphant entry into Jerusalem corresponds to the 10th of Nissan on the Jewish calendar, which is five days before the Passover. I was fascinated when I found out that it is the day the Jews bring the lambs they are going to sacrifice for the Passover into Jerusalem. How fitting it is that this is also the exact day and time that the Ultimate Sacrificial Lamb, the Lamb of God, who takes away the sin of the world, enters Jerusalem. Around 1500 years earlier, just before the Jews were released from their slavery in Egypt, God commanded them to sacrifice a lamb. This lamb was a sign of release from bondage and sin, so that when Christ came to save the Israelites they would recognise Him and realise He is the Messiah.

As was the case throughout all of Jesus' life, the Pharisees were not happy about this event and shouted for Jesus to stop the crowds from worshiping Him. But Jesus turns to them and says, "if I stop the crowds from worshiping Me, the rocks themselves would shout out and worship." As usual, the Pharisees had no response and walked away angered saying, "We have accomplished nothing. Look the whole world has gone after Him."

What the Fathers Say

"Although He came as a poor person lacking glory, yet the crowds welcomed Him as a King and Savior of Israel. They perceived that He was the righteous King who came in the name of the Lord (Ps 2:6). They accepted His kingdom wholeheartedly, and they expressed their feelings by shouting "Hosanna!" or 'Hoshaana' which means 'He has redeemed us'."

– Fr Tadros Y Malaty

Liturgical

In matins a great procession, known as the Procession of the Cross, takes place. In this procession, 12 psalms and gospels are read from various stations around the church. The same procession is done on the feast of the cross.

During the liturgy, readings are taken from each of the four Gospels each of which give a different but true perspective of Christ: Matthew quotes Old Testament prophecies to highlight that Christ is the Messiah and King; Mark shows that Christ is authoritative as the Son of God; Luke places emphasis on His ministry and redemption to all people as the Son of Man; and John highlights that through Him, the divine Son of God, we are granted eternal life. Thus by reading from the four gospels we receive a full account while reminding ourselves of these significant characteristics of Christ.

People, Places and Things

Bethany

Bethany is a town located on the Mount of Olives. Bethany was "about two miles" southeast of Jerusalem, a journey taking a total of about 55 minutes by foot. It is here that Jesus spent His final nights before His crucifixion.

Who were the Romans?

The Romans were the people who controlled Israel at the time of Christ. They required of the Jews high taxes and Roman officers often mistreated the Jews. The romans put their own governors or procurators over all of Israel; Pontius Pilate is an example of a procurator put in place

Many of the hymns and responses on this day are about the royalty of Christ the King, but as one of the responses says, "He who sits on the Cherubim, rode on a colt and entered Jerusalem. What a great act of humility!" Christ left His high place for our sake, to enter our hearts.

Directly after the liturgy a special funeral service is prayed, known as the general funeral prayers. The entire congregation attends this service and at its conclusion, the priest sprinkles the congregation with the water which has been prayed over during the funeral service. This is because during Holy Week no funeral services are conducted. This is done so as not to detract from the focus of the week, the sufferings of Christ, and we do not share in any other grief.

by the Roman Empire. By law, if a Roman soldier asked a Jew to carry his bag, which was often very heavy, and walk with him for a mile, the Jew would have to do it or else he would be punished. This rule was rather difficult for the Jews and it almost became oppressive. Thus when Christ taught to go the extra mile, many of His listeners were shocked, as Christ was indirectly teaching them to love and aid those who oppressed them.

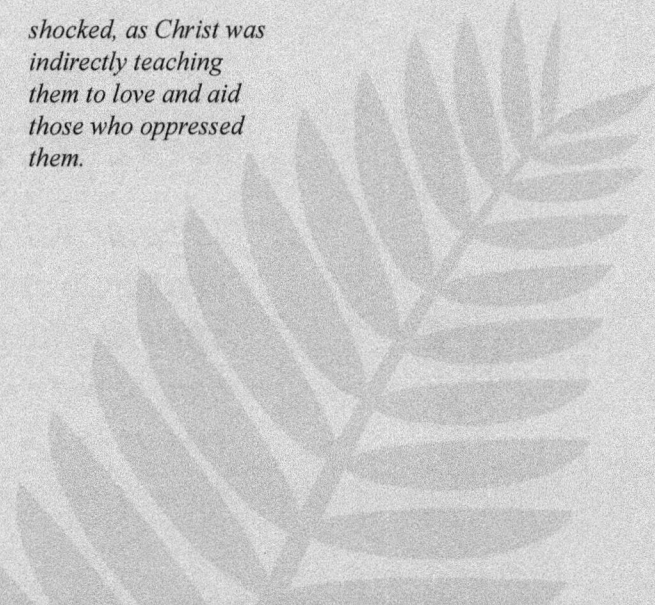

COLT OR DONKEY?

The Gospel of Matthew tells us that the disciples were sent to get Jesus both a colt and a donkey. So which one did the Lord ride?

Well St John Chrysostom, as well as other Church Fathers, tell us that Jesus rode on both. This was to fulfil the prophecy spoken by Ezekiel the prophet, "Behold, your King is coming to you; He is just and having salvation, lowly and riding on a donkey, a colt, the foal of a donkey." The prophecy does not just speak of the Lord entering on a donkey, but on both.

The donkey is often associated with the stubborn Jewish people who throughout history disobeyed God. Even at the time of Jesus many were stubborn toward Him. On the other hand, the colt on which no one had ever ridden represents the Gentiles, people to whom God had not yet revealed Himself yet who are humble, obedient and accepting of His Word, Jesus Christ our Lord.

Reflections

Imagine you are the donkey; would you attribute the glory the people were showing to you or to Christ?

MONDAY EVE

Events

MONDAY EVE

Jesus spent the days of this week in Jerusalem, and at night He would stay at Bethany. On this night, Christ tells of His upcoming death and resurrection.

Monday eve is the night the church takes us through various occasions where Jesus explicitly says that He will be killed. The first story appears in the 1st hour of Monday eve. The Gospel tells us the story of a group of Greeks who wanted to meet Jesus. So the Greeks approached Phillip, who with Andrew went to Christ and told Him of the Greeks who wanted to meet Him. However, Jesus seemed distracted, and His response was quite strange to the disciples, almost as if His mind were somewhere else. Snapping out of His thoughts, Jesus tells the disciples that time is up. He is about to be glorified, but in order for this glorification to take place, He must first die. He says that if He were to stay on earth and not die then both He and us would be alone forever, but if He dies then He and us can live together forever!

People, Places and Things

Jerusalem

The capital city of Israel was moved to Jerusalem by King David the prophet, thus why it may also be referred to as the city of David. It was chosen by king David for its strategic location, high on a plateau in the hills of Judah, giving it great advantage in times of war. It later became the location of the great temple that King Solomon built for the Lord

Simon Peter

Simon Peter was a disciple of Jesus. Simon is the brother of Andrew

Jesus goes on to say that if you love this world and put it first in your life then you cannot be with Him. If anyone wants to serve the Lord, they will need to follow Him, and those who serve the Lord, the Father will honour. It is quite a smack in the face. Neither Phillip nor Andrew can work out what is going on or why Jesus was saying what He was saying. They just concluded that they missed something, or that Jesus was tired and a little dazed, and didn't really know what He was saying. But soon they will understand all of what the Lord just spoke.

In the Gospel of the 3rd and 9th hours we read the famous story when Jesus asks His disciples "Who do men say that I am?" and Simon Peter with his ever-famous confession of faith responds

and the son of a man named John, hence Jesus has been noted as calling him "Simon bar-Jonah" (Simon, son of John). He was seen in the early church as the leader and spokesperson of the Twelve Apostles but was not higher ranked. His actual name was Simon, or Simeon in Hebrew but was named Peter, which means rock, after his famous confession that Jesus is "The Christ, the Son of the Living God" (as seen in the Gospels of the 3rd, 6th and 9th hours of Monday eve of the Holy Pascha). He is also called Cephas by St Paul, which also means rock. Tradition holds that Peter was to be crucified as Christ was, but he protested and said that he was not worthy to die in the same way as his Master Jesus Christ died. He thus requested to be crucified upside down and was martyred by being crucified upside down.

What the Fathers Say

"But see how carefully and wisely He instructs them at the right time. For He neither told them these things at the beginning, so He would not worry them; nor at the time itself, so He would not confound them. But they had received sufficient proof of His power, when He had given them promises that were very great concerning life everlasting, then He introduces also what He had to say concerning these things, once and twice and often interweaving it with His miracles and His instructions."

— St John Chrysostom

saying, "You are the Christ, the Son of the Living God." This section of the story is discussed often in sermons and books, but the section that is generally overlooked is what Christ then says after: "the Son of Man must suffer many things, and be rejected by the elders and chief priests and scribes, and be killed, and be raised the third day."

This conversation between Jesus and His disciples is much deeper than it appears. This conversation took place in Caeserea Phillipi, north of Jerusalem. Caeserea Phillipi had a strong history of pagan worship, and still had it deeply rooted in their culture. At the time, Caesar Augustus declared himself a god and the son of a god, and many of the locals of Caeserea Phillipi were patrons of this idea. The locals built shrines and altars for Caesar and were diligent in their belief. Thus when Jesus asks "Who do men say that I am?," He is alluding to not only Caesar not being the son of god, but also pointing to Himself as the true Son of God. Peter's response is perfect. He says that Jesus is the Messiah, the Christ, and the Son of the living God! This statement shows that Jesus is not only the Christ and the Messiah that the Jews were waiting for, but that He is also the Son of the living God, which the rest of the world have been waiting for too. Peter thus declares the truth that Jesus is the true God of all, Jews and Gentiles alike, and that Caesar and all others are not.

The rest of the Gospel readings for this night also cover the Lord's prophecies of how He is to be betrayed, suffer, die and rise again.

What the Fathers Say

"It is altogether necessary for Him to undergo His saving Passion for us and to suffer the violence of the Jews."

– St Cyril of Alexandria

Reflections

Put yourself in Peter's shoes, and ask yourself this question, "Who do you say that I AM?"…Who is Jesus to you?

Liturgical

Church Pascha services begin this night. All the tunes are said in the sad mournful tune and the services are prayed without opening the sanctuary and are conducted entirely outside the choir section of the church. This is because the sanctuary represents Jerusalem and Christ suffered and was crucified outside of Jerusalem "therefore let us go forth to Him, outside the gate, bearing His reproach" (Hebrews 13:13). Around the church, black veils with crosses are hung up and placed on the lecterns.

There are five nightly hours and five daily hours. For the sake of convenience, in local churches these are prayed together over two sessions, the 5 daily are prayed in the morning and the 5 nightly are prayed in the evening. The hours correspond to modern hours as seen in the table below. These prayers replace the daily hours of the Agpia and all prayers are focused solely on those in the Pascha services. During every hour, readings are taken from the Old Testament (prophecies and psalms) followed by a Gospel reading.

Daily/Nightly Hours	Corresponding Time
1st	6 AM
3rd	9 AM
6th	12 PM
9th	3 PM
11th	5 PM

MONDAY

Events

MONDAY

On Monday, Jesus journeys from Bethany, the place where He was staying, to the temple in Jerusalem. On the way He got hungry and in the distance He could see a fig tree that had leaves on it. Now the fig tree isn't like any other fruit tree. It only produces leaves when it has fruits so that it can cover and protect the fruits from the sun and predators such as birds. However, this was not the case. As Jesus came closer and inspected the tree and its leaves, He could not find any fruit. This didn't make Jesus very happy so he cursed the fig tree in front of all His disciples.

The Jewish leaders had so much pride in knowing the laws and statutes of God that they forgot the point of the law. They spent so much time focusing on how good they were because they knew the law that they forgot the God of the law. So while they had the appearance of, and spoke as those following the law, they did not bear any fruit from their knowledge of the law. Thus, like the fig tree, they bore the leaves and had the knowledge of the will of God, but they did not practise the statutes of God and therefore did not bear any fruit. They only had the appearance of bearing fruit. Nothing caused Jesus to become as angry as the pride and hypocrisy of the leaders. For if the leaders were behaving as they were, how were the people supposed to behave any differently? The fig tree with leaves but no fruit is a type of the Jewish leaders. Jesus in His incredible love does not curse or destroy the leaders, but the tree. For if the tree just reminded Him of the Jews and He reacted by destroying the tree, how much more angry was He with the Jews? But out of His incredible love for the

Jews, He destroyed the tree in their place, as a sign for them. But they did not learn.

Thus the Lord feels the same pain when we know to do good and do not do it. At these moments, we are the same as the tree and the same as the unrighteous leaders of the Jews. Yet just as Christ destroyed the tree instead of the Jews, so for our salvation He destroyed His own pure and innocent body instead of our death- deserving selves, all for the great love He has for us.

Therefore, no matter how much we know to do good, we will never bear fruit without the practise of good. Just because you know how good an apple is for you, you will never have the benefits of the apple until you eat it. The Jewish leaders knew the commands of God, but did not receive the nutrients of the good because they did not practise the commands of God.

JESUS IN THE TEMPLE

After this, the Lord and His disciples went on their way to the temple and Jesus saw something else that really upset Him. People were buying and selling and had turned the holy temple of the Most High God into a market place! Jesus became very angry and in a holy and zealous response, released the doves and animals of the sellers. He also turned over the tables of the money changers and rebuked them saying, "My house is a house of prayer for all nations. But you have made it a den of thieves." The priests, scribes and Pharisees heard this and were humiliated as the keeping of the holy

What the Fathers Say

"Our Lord knows all that dwells in our hearts, He wants us to beware at this time not to pay attention to exterior appearances only, but to make sure that we build up our spiritual lives as well, so that we may live in the presence of God."

– H.G. Bishop Angelos

temple was their responsibility. In response, they began to seek out "how they might destroy Him, for they feared Him," that He would damage their esteem in the eyes of the people.

There are two clear points to take away from this story. First, our sometimes disregard for the holy places. One of the ways that many of us disrespect the holy places (the Church) is when we talk in church. Did you know that there is a church canon that says "No one shall talk and converse at the time of the prayers and the liturgy except on a subject of religion and the readings, wherein is salvation of souls; and they shall be silent at the hearing of the precepts of the Lord – Praise be to Him – until the liturgy is finished." – 4th Canon, Canons of Christodulus, Patriarch of Alexandria (1047 – 1077 AD).

Secondly, not to value the praise of men over the praise of God. The Jewish leaders wanted to get rid of Jesus, not because He was wrong (as interpreters of the law, they knew the law and that He was right) but because He shamed and embarrassed them. They did not want people to think less of them. They desired the praise of the people more than the praise of God. This is clear.

Many times in Jesus' ministry He told His followers to beware of the leaven of the Pharisees, and to not fast the way the leaders fasted. The Pharisees showed the world they were fasting by making themselves ill and dehydrated, acting faint, all to show how great their fast was to the

What the Fathers Say

"Truly, when He came and found no fruit in (the Jews), he cursed them through the fig tree, saying, 'Let there be henceforth no fruit from you;' and the fig tree was dead and fruitless so that even the disciples wondered when it withered away…"

- St Athanasius

people and not out of love for God. Christ even warned the people not to pray as their leaders did, who would proclaim aloud saying how great and sinless they were compared to others. How wrong they were and Jesus made this clear! Many were ignorant and believed in the appearance of holiness of the priests and the Pharisees. But Christ opened the eyes of the people and exposed the true nature of the leaders.

Many say that it is fine for them to do as they please because God is merciful and kind and quick to forgive and truly He is. But the Lord is a just judge! If you have done wrong, and have not repented then there will be a consequence, even if you claim to love God, for the Lord says, "As many as I love, I rebuke and chasten." – Rev 3:19

So do not think you are free from the consequence of your sins because you follow God. He made it very clear that there will be a consequence; He even showed how He feels in His cleansing of the temple. The Lord clearly showed that we should have reverence and respect for the Most High's dwelling, or else be prepared for chastisement, not because He hates you, but because He wants you to be holy as He is holy, because He really does love you.

Likewise, many of us esteem ourselves very highly, often more than each other. When someone wrongs us, we believe that we have the right to retaliate, to fight or to speak evil of that person. But where is our humility? Christ Himself

What the Fathers Say

"...The Lord cursed them under the figure of the fig tree. And yet, He still spared them in His loving-kindness, and did not destroy the root and the entire tree. For He did not curse the root, but said that no man will eat fruit of it henceforth. When He did this, He abolished the shadow, causing it to wither; but preserved the root, so that we might not be grafted upon it; 'they too, if they abide not in unbelief, may attain to be grafted into their own olive tree.'"

– St Athanasius

told us to turn the other cheek, to walk the extra mile, to pray for those who harm us and to love those who hate us! In so doing these things we will become "perfect, just as your Father in heaven is perfect." – Matt 5:48.

We also get annoyed when those around us speak rumours or say nasty things concerning us. It may be difficult to ignore, but why should we worry about what people say about us? Why are we so concerned about what others say over what God says?

A young monk once asked St Macarius the Great for some advice on how to live a good and holy life. St Macarius told him to go to the cemetery and rebuke and curse and throw stones at those in the graves. The young monk did so and returned. St Macarius then told him to go praise and speak

People, Places and Things

"Certain Greeks"

Given that St John mentions these Greeks at the time of a feast, and given that they were in the temple when seeking Jesus, it is assumed that the Greeks spoken of by St John in the Gospel of the 1st hour were more than likely proselytes or at least in the process of becoming proselytes. A Proselyte is a person who converts from non-Jewish beliefs to the Jewish faith and has completed the rituals to become Jews, i.e. circumcision, rites of purification, etc.

Philip

Philip was one of the twelve Apostles. Philip was the disciple who called Nathaniel (another of the twelve apostles) to "come and see" Jesus. Philip is also famously known for asking Jesus if he and the others could see the Father.

highly to those in the graves. Again the young monk did so and returned. St Macarius then asked the young monk, "When you cursed and spoke roughly to them, what did they do?" The young monk replied, "Nothing." Then St Macarius said, "And when you spoke praise and complimented them, how did they react?" Again, the young monk said, "Nothing." Finally, St Macarius reached his point and told the young monk, "Go and do likewise; when people curse you, do nothing and when people praise you, do nothing."

This is the attitude every Christian should aim to have, so that we may give glory to God, and inherit the incredible life that endures forever. Let us not be as the Jews were, who broke the heart of God, who mistreated His love for them. Rather, let us be as Christ requests of us, holy and humble in heart.

What the Fathers Say

"We can only bear fruit if God is in our lives."

- H.G Bishop Angelos

Andrew

Andrew is also one of the twelve. He was originally a disciple of John the Baptist. Andrew was one of the first disciples of Jesus. He also led his brother Simon Peter to Jesus. Both Simon and Andrew were fishermen by trade. Andrew brought the "lad" with the five loaves and the two fish to Jesus and Jesus fed the 5000 men. The last mention of Andrew bar-Jonah is in the Book of Acts. It is believed that Andrew was martyred on an X-shaped cross.

Money Changers

The temple had its own currency because the Roman currency had Caesar's image engraved on it and no graven images were allowed in the temple. There was therefore a need for the temple to have its own currency and thus moneychangers. It acted more as a modern day foreign exchange. They were to exchange the currencies of the travellers, and even the locals, for the locals used Roman currency at that time. At the time of Jesus, the money changers were also fairly corrupt and would not give fair exchanges, often taking more than was honest.

Liturgical

All prayers since last night have been in a mournful (sad) tune to remind us of Jesus' passion. As in the nightly hours, the Pascha praise is prayed each hour before the psalm. This praise, "To You is the power, and the glory, and the blessing, and the honour forever. Amen...", dedicated to this special and difficult journey is chanted 12 times every hour, 6 times by each side of the church with the corresponding verses. This chant is recited with the angels in heaven as it is on earth: "Blessing and honour and glory and power be to Him who sits on the throne and to the Lamb, forever and ever!" (Revelations 5:13).

In the mornings, the day litanies are prayed at the conclusion of the service with prostrations (metanoina) as the church is fasting and abstaining. It has been the practice of the church to make prostration only on empty stomach. During the night litanies most people would have eaten therefore there are no prostrations.

Reflections

What are the fruits in my life, and what are the leaves? Are the leaves there to protect the fruit or to hide its fruitlessness?

TUESDAY EVE

TUESDAY EVE

The Gospel of the 3rd hour begins with one person asking Christ if only a few people will be saved. However Jesus turns and says to him, don't focus on numbers or if many will be saved or not, rather focus on how to be saved. Do not focus on who will be saved, but on how you will be saved, and to be saved we must enter through the narrow gate. To relate this to our world today, we often speak about why God isn't bringing everyone to our classes or youth to our meetings, and we fear that it is all unfruitful. However, we should rather speak of what we can do to bring these services to God. Throughout the bible we see God bringing salvation with the smallest amounts of people. So instead of explaining how to bring numbers to God, Jesus teaches how to bring our hearts to Him.

I believe the narrow way spoken of by Christ can mean filtering out things that unconsciously harm us. We look around at the world today and wonder how certain people are able to do certain things, whether it's criminal offenses like violent and abusive behaviour, stealing, or even those "legal" sins which are very destructive to our salvation, such as pornography, drunkenness, and sexual acts. There is no doubt that at younger ages, you would have never even thought you were capable of doing such things! So what happened?

Simply put, we need to put a filter on the things that we allow to influence us and eventually dictates a way of life that does not necessarily suit as a Christian. Things like, friends, social media, TV shows etc indirectly dictates certain behaviour and moral values that we as Christian do not agree with yet over time what used to be foreign to our eyes and ears is now acceptable. Especially that some of these influences come in nicely wrapped up packages, for example a cool group of friends or a funny TV show or the popularity someone might get from the number of likes they have on a social media.

You might ask what does this have to do with the narrow gate? I tell you it has everything... filtering these influences often comes at a price... going along with a group of cool friends whom their words and actions far from glorifies God will cost me to be "unpopular." Not watching a TV show that I know will slowly change my Christian principles will come at the cost of being left out of a conversation at school. Today Christ warns us

What the Fathers Say

"I came as a hen to protect them, but they received Me in hatred and betrayal, I came as a mother, and they assumed I came to kill them, so they killed Me."

– St Jerome

What the Fathers Say

"In fact, if we scrutinise all our readings we will find them about this subject matter. Our Saviour warns us against hypocrisy!"

– Fr Bishoy Kamel

exactly about that saying: "Enter by the narrow gate; for wide is the gate and broad is the way that leads to destruction, and there are many who go in by it. Because narrow is the gate and difficult is the way which leads to life, and there are few who find it" - Mat 7: 13-14. We note here that He gave us a warning about the numbers

Wide Gate = Many who go in by it
Narrow Gate = Few who find it

So lets not be surprised when we follow the commandments to find ourselves among "the few who find it"

People, Places and Things

Who are the Pharisees?

The Pharisees are a Jewish sect that is believed to have begun in about 160 – 143 B.C, during the leadership of Jonathan Maccabeus. They were established during a time when the Jewish laws were in jeopardy of being destroyed. Hence, they were put in place to preserve the law. The word Pharisees means "the separated ones" and this was in regard to three types of separation: separation from people, separation from pagan practises, and separating themselves to the study of the law. They were the most influential Jewish sect in the New Testament.

You may notice that after the litanies the congregation chants "Kerieleyson" or "Lord have mercy" twelve times before "Epouro" or "O' King of Peace". It is said that the twelve Kerieleyson's are an additional means of cleansing ourselves spiritually from our sins in preparation for the great feast at the end of the week, the joyous Resurrection. Tradition also holds that the hymn "O' King of peace" was one of the hymns martyrs would sing while being persecuted and being put to death. The chant is particularly reflective and as such lets go home from this pascha service with a take home message that though Christ is going through this violent passion yet He is the King of peace and that He will give us His peace and forgive us our sins.

Liturgical

Reflections

How serious are you about keeping a filter over things that influence you? What do you do now that you never would have done a few years ago?

TUESDAY

Events

TUESDAY

Although it is not mentioned in the hourly Gospels of Tuesday, today we commemorate Jesus and His disciples passing by the Fig tree, which Christ had cursed the previous day. As they passed it, they saw that it was completely withered away. "Now in the morning, as they passed by, they saw the fig tree dried up from the roots." – Mark 11:21. This is quite miraculous, as the fig tree is not a small shrub, but is a large tree. So for the tree to be completely withered, after only one day, is entirely miraculous. Jesus' message however, is of much more importance then the miracle itself. The message continues from that of Monday's. On Monday we saw that God despises hypocrisy, pride and those who desire the praise of men above the praise of God.

Tuesday is a particularly interesting day. It seems to be just as Tuesday eve in that Jesus is still prophesying about His death, but in fact we notice that Jesus is building up to something and that He is revealing more and more about Himself to his followers.

The Gospel of the first hour starts off with the Lord speaking very mysteriously to a crowd of people, telling them that He is going somewhere and where He is going no one is able to go with Him. Some of the people therefore thought that He was going to kill Himself!?! Jesus then, with full authority yet in His tender way, highlights that the people are so limited in their understanding, that they are from earth and He is from Heaven and that if they don't believe in Him, they will die in their sins. So the people ask Jesus, "Who are You?" It seems as though the people knew or at least suspected who Jesus was, but were not fully willing to believe it. How could they not know? Every prophecy ever spoken of by the prophets was being fulfilled by this incredible Man!

Who else can muster up great crowds all day every day just to hear Him speak? Who else was able to heal the blind, the deaf, the lame, and the mute? Who else could raise the dead, give sight to one born blind, restore the lepers, and feed the thousands from the smallest amount of food? Who else could raise a man to life, four days after he died? Who else could be the most loved and hated person in Israel at the same time. Who else but Jesus the Messiah, the Son of the living God!

Although Jesus never actually said that He was the Messiah, the people all knew that He very well could be The Anointed One. All Jesus said is that He is the same person He claimed to be from the beginning of His ministry.

A common question crosses the minds of many people – "Why didn't He just say, I am the Christ, the Saviour of the world!" Well, let us imagine He does say that.... who would believe Him? If the richest man on earth sat next to you on the train and said to you he was the richest man on earth, would you believe him? Of course you wouldn't! Why would the richest man on earth speak to you so casually, and more than that, why would he catch the train in the first place, he should be in his helicopter, or some super car, or some magic teleporting machine or something like that, not the train.

The same concept applies to Jesus. He could very well have just told the people that He was the Christ, the Messiah, but no one would have believed Him. So instead, He had to prove it! And He did! Every time He opened His mouth, every time He lifted His hands, every time He was sad, and every time He smiled or laughed, He proved it in all His coming in and going out. He truly did prove that He was the Christ, the Son of the Living God! But the people still did not believe. Their hearts were hardened, hence Christ's mildly frustrated and truly saddened response, "Just what I have been saying to you from the beginning."

Jesus then, knowing that they would not understand, tells them bluntly that He is from the "Father." So Jesus says again, "When you lift up the Son of Man, then you will know that I am He." Jesus is now beginning to be more detailed with His prophecy regarding His death. When He says that He must be lifted up, He is clearly building towards something, but the climax is not yet. Jesus said that He is from the "Father" but the people did not understand. While it may seem obvious to us now what Jesus was saying, you have to understand that back then, and in fact in the entire Old Testament, God was never referred to as Father! Thus, by Jesus saying He was from the Father was such a strange thing to them. They had never heard that word in its divine context before. Thus, while many wanted to follow Him, their limited human understanding held them back.

In the third and sixth hour Gospels, Jesus tells us how the hardened hearts of the chosen Jewish people has truly caused deep anguish and sadness to the heart of God, and in the ninth hour Gospel, Jesus warns us of the signs of the coming apocalypse and what will take place. But the highlight of the Tuesday of Holy Week is the Gospel of the eleventh hour.

The Gospel of the eleventh hour, taken from the account of St Matthew, starts off with Christ telling His famous parable of the talents. The moral of this parable is: be ready! You do not know when the end will come! Do not waste your time! Do not be lazy! Use the gifts God has given you so that when you are to give account of your life on the Day of Judgement, you may have something good and Holy to present before the Just Judge, and He may find you worthy to see what no eye has seen and to hear what no ear has heard.

Much contemplation on the parable of the talents has been told, and great messages have been learnt. How all are given gifts, and all are told to work with what they have been given. However, many people, both youth and adults take this to mean that only the priests and servants of the church have these gifts, and only they have been

What the Fathers Say

"Actually, we are the Jerusalem that Jesus wept over. After we came to know the mysteries of the Truth, the words of the Gospel, and the teachings of the church; and after we have seen the mysteries of the Lord, we still commit sins! The Lord wept over our Jerusalem due to our sin."

– Origen.

called to serve. Origen, a second century Christian scholar says, "It is fitting not only for the Saviour to take up His Cross but also for us to carry it, doing compulsory service for our salvation."

If service is compulsory, then clearly we all have been given gifts of service, and perhaps we are just lazy and make excuses to avoid serving the Lord. When the King of kings and Lord of lords asks you to serve, then you serve! He is not asking you to serve because He needs you, but because He wants to work through you! He is yearning to bless you and will use any excuse to do so! So give Him a reason! Believe me, you will get more out of serving Him then He will ever get from you. Do you think you can do something that the Master Creator can't? So if you think that only the strong are called to serve, then rethink the parable of the talents. Did Jesus ever say that He gave the most talents to the strong?

We often think that the person with the most talents was more blessed or capable than the person with the least, but history shows us otherwise. God so often, would bless and qualify those who were called rather then call those who are naturally gifted. God chose the stutterer Moses to be the greatest leader in Jewish history; the small fragile shepherd boy David to be a mighty warrior and the king of Israel. He chose Simon Peter, the denier of God, to convert thousands with a single sermon and He chose Saul the murderer and persecutor to be Paul the most active and influential apostle to the Gentile world.

And today, God chooses you! A young individual! To do so many things through!

So what if God actually gives more to the weaker person, and less to the more capable? The action that pleased God in the parable was not that one doubled his share of talents and the other didn't, it was that one trusted in God rather than his own abilities. Often, the more capable are unable to trust in God like the less capable, that's why God often elects the weaker rather than the strong; those who are poor in spirit and humble in heart.

What if God gives more talents to the weaker person to cover his weaknesses, and in knowing this, and understanding the origin of these talents, the weaker person trusts more in God than any qualified person ever could. What if God gives fewer talents to the strong person, who in thinking themself capable to do all without God, fail!

We are all weak, but what makes us truly strong is our ability to submit to God, and truly, only a person who trusts in God can do this!

So, when you see your elders, servants and faithful youth fall, know that they, as well as us all, are truly weak, despite all the blessings and talents. Know this, that above all, what makes us truly blessed and talented is our desire to rise when we fall, to fight the good fight and to finish the race. To trust in God is the greatest strength, and all that you need for service is to trust in the Servant King.

From all the readings of this day, it is clear that Jesus is building up to something, and it isn't until the last word, of the last verse, of the last Gospel of the day that this climax is revealed.

After much teaching, instructing and debate, Jesus reveals to all listening that He, the Son of the living God, the Almighty One, is to be crucified. To the disciples, this was impossible, as Jesus was to save them from the Romans. How could He save them yet be crucified by the Romans?

Jesus reveals that He, the Everlasting, the Timeless, the Holy, the Infinite, the Source of all Glory, the Creator of the universe, the Son of the Living God, the Second Person of the Holy Trinity, is not just to be betrayed, not just to suffer, and not just to be killed by the ones He loves, but that they will completely mutilate Him and crucify Him. Doesn't seem like a big climax to you? Well that's

People, Places and Things

Talent

A talent was a system of measurement of money. A weight, the most basic of which was called a shekel, was used to equal an amount of gold or precious mineral, and that is how value would be appointed to a weight. A shekel was the basic unit of weight in the Hebrew money system. One talent was roughly equal to about 35 kg, which equated to about 3000 shekels.

Gentiles

Gentiles are those who are not Jewish by birth and are not part of the Jewish faith. There are Gentiles who convert to Judaism. They are called proselytes.

probably because you already know how the story ends...but try and think back to the first time you ever heard of what crucifixion actually was, and that Jesus went through all that. Well, that's how it was for Jesus' most faithful followers. For the first time ever, He bluntly reveals to His disciples, without any parable or figurative language, that He was going to be crucified.

Now let's put this into perspective. The disciples have now been following Jesus for about three years. In that time they have seen the impossible happen. Roaring winds and raging waters, by a word, were calmed to paralysed stillness! The entire concept of science and physics was dissolved the moment they saw Him walk on water! The concept of a terminal disease no longer existed in their minds because they knew, no matter what you had, Jesus can fix it! From His mouth came words that would bring tears of joy and repentance to the smiling faces of loved sinners, and uncontrollable laughter from the innocent mouths of babies and children! Then all of a sudden, this same Man speaks of His crucifixion?

They witnessed Jesus creating eyes for the man born blind! Defy all cultural custom by showing love to the Samaritan woman! Heal the infirmities of a man paralysed for 38 years! And now the one in the same Man tells of His upcoming sufferings, death, and resurrection. To the disciples, this was impossible!

It is at this time the disciples begin to notice

the behaviour of Jesus change just slightly. They notice that He is still the same incredible and loving being that He always was, but His teachings start to change from teachings of how to live for God, and of the Truth, to teachings of the end of the world, and His death.

The disciples are now confused and assume, as was often the case, that they did not understand what Jesus was really teaching them and thus partially dismissed what Jesus was saying as a hidden message they once again did not understand. One portion of their hearts believed what He was saying concerning His death as true, and that He really was going to suffer and die, but Jesus does not really get into the details of what was going to happen to Him, the disciples leaned toward the belief that they are just confused and are not really getting the message. Nevertheless, as with all things, there was some part of the disciples' hearts that took His prophecy of suffering and death for truth. Jesus kept speaking of His sufferings and that began to create fear, doubt and paranoia in their hearts. And fear, doubt and paranoia, if undealt with, will grow until it becomes consuming! This became the case with Christ's closest friends.

So when finally Christ straight out says that He is going to be crucified, all the fear, doubt and paranoia that was built up in the disciples exploded all at once, and from this point onward, it seems as though the attitude of the disciples changes from a mighty untouchable attitude, to a truly vulnerable one. Not only did it start to sink in that their Master may actually die, but that He was going to be murdered in the worst and most foul way known to people of that age, and of any age till today. The King of kings and Lord of lords was to be crucified. While the disciples were planning to crown Him King, the Jewish elders were planning to kill Him.

It is for this reason that the psalm of the eleventh hour is Psalm 45:6, "Your throne O God is forever and ever; a sceptre of righteousness is the sceptre of Your kingdom."

Liturgical

All of the hymns and chants of this week are beautiful but one in particular, chanted today, "Pekethronos" or "Your throne", the psalm of the 11th hour stands out. It is chanted in its special melody known as the "Shami" tune.

Although at times it seems mournful, it is a royal tune which has many variations. While listening to the tune you feel at times it pushes your emotions down and makes you feel sad, while at other times you feel it is a playful and joyful tune. If you listen carefully you will notice that the tune builds up a few times before it anticlimaxes, time and time again, as it goes on and on, and as such we feel the truth behind the words – that God's throne is "forever and ever." We imagine our Lord sitting on His throne, judging the world with righteousness, justice and power.

On this day, at the 11th hour, the 2nd part of "To You is the power" is added which says "My Good Saviour". This is added to highlight the Gospel readings where Christ mentions that He will die and that He will save the whole world.

Reflections

Time is one of the talents that we are given by God. How much of this talent do we use to bring fruits that are worthy to be presented to Him?

WEDNESDAY EVE

Events

WEDNESDAY EVE

As Jesus mostly did leading up to His death, He spoke to His disciples about the end of the world and His upcoming death and resurrection, yet for the most part they did not understand. Wednesday eve goes through much of what Jesus taught and spoke concerning the Kingdom of Heaven and the end of the world. He also further rebukes the Pharisees.

One of the parables the Lord speaks is mentioned in the Gospel of the first hour. It is the story of the marriage feast for the king's son.

The story goes that the son of the king was to get married and the king was set to hold a feast for him. So he sent out his servants to go and invite all the noble families, the rich, the politicians and all the rulers of the land. So the servants went out and invited everyone. But they would not come and they made excuses. They ignored the servants and went back to their farms and businesses. Worst of all, some even captured the servants, insulted and mistreated them, and even killed them. But when the king found out what the people had done to his servants, "he was furious". The king sent out his armies and destroyed those who murdered the king's servants and rejected the king's invitation. The feast was ready, but those who were invited were not worthy, so the king sent out other servants to go out to all the land and go and invite all they saw; all the bad and the good, the poor, the sick, all whom they saw. So the servants did so and the feast was filled with all kinds of people from all over the land. The king was happy. However, when he saw a man present who was not dressed appropriately, and the man was speechless as to why he was dressed so inappropriately, the king orders that the man be bound and thrown out of the feast.

This story is fairly strange but once explained, makes perfect sense. The king represents God; the servants are all the prophets and holy men and women who came before Christ and taught of the Holy ways of God; the feast is the glorious kingdom of heaven and the partaking of the Body and Blood of Jesus Christ. The rich, the noble, and all those who were originally invited is a symbol of the Jewish people, who were the chosen people of God, but they rejected God and His Son Jesus Christ and the glorious kingdom of heaven, and they were lazy and made excuses and lost all that they were offered by God. The poor the sick and all those who accepted the invitation are the Gentiles, all the non-Jews who accepted the word of God and His glorious kingdom. However, not all who attend the feast can stay and enjoy the feast as was the case with the man who was not wearing the wedding garment. In the days of Christ, wedding garments were handed out to the guests of the feast by those who stood by the entrances, thus if someone was not wearing a wedding garment, then they did not enter the feast from the entrances and were most likely not invited and thus tried to sneak in. The man who was cast out because he was not dressed appropriately represents all those believers who say they are Christian, but do not show any proof of this. They claim to be Christians, but neither their words nor their actions testify of their apparent belief and

What the Fathers Say

"He says to His disciples, "Let your waists be girded and your lamps burning." The girded waists is virginity; the "burning lamps" are good works; the oil is God's gift of our conscience, which dwells in our hearts."

– St Augustine

thus they try and sneak in to Heaven by their own means. Therefore, even many who claim to be Christian will be thrown into "outer darkness."

Another parable mentioned this night is the parable of the ten virgins. Five virgins are wise and the other virgins are foolish. They all take lamps and prepare to go to a wedding feast, alluding to Judgment Day and the kingdom of Heaven. The wise took oil for their lamps, just in case they were going to wait a long time for the bridegroom to come, but the foolish did not prepare themselves for the delay. Alas, the bridegroom was delayed so all slept and relaxed. Then, all of a sudden, at midnight, while all were unaware, a loud call was heard and proclaimed that the bridegroom was coming. The foolish looked at their lamps and realised that they had run out of oil, so they asked the wise for some oil, but they did not have enough to spare. The foolish had no choice but

People, Places and Things

Parables

Parables are stories that have a deep-rooted message. They often compare scenarios or objects for the purpose of getting the message across. Parables are known to be very visual and involve many things from its modern day surroundings. Notice how many of the parables of Jesus relate to farming. This is because many of the people and much of the economy at the time had a big involvement in farming. The greatest theme Jesus used in His parables was about the Kingdom of God. The use of parables was very common even before the time of Christ. When God wanted to teach King David a lesson He sent the prophet Nathan to tell David a parable.

to go and buy oil for their lamps. The foolish then returned to the wedding feast and they found that everyone else had entered and only they were left outside in the dark. So the foolish knocked on the door. The bridegroom answered. The foolish said "Here we are friend, allow us into the feast! "But the bridegroom, looking at them in confusion says, "I do not know you." The foolish reply, "But we were invited." The bridegroom declares, "Then why didn't you come when you were summoned; assuredly I say to you I do not know you!"

Once again the parable seems a little strange, but once explained, is very beautiful and has a very powerful message. The bridegroom is a symbol of Jesus, and the feast is the kingdom of heaven. The wise virgins are those who hear, and follow the word of God with all their hearts and practice good deeds. Thus, their lamps are full. The foolish are those who hear the word, claim to be Christians but do not have the works and actions to prove their belief. Thus, their lamps are empty.

The eleventh hour Gospel is the climax of the evening. It was close to the day of Passover, and all the leaders of the Jews gathered to purify themselves. And as they looked around, they noticed that Jesus was not around preaching. So they debated whether or not He would come to the feast. At this point they had given a command that if anyone knew where He was, "he should report it, that they might seize Him" (John 11:57). It is clear, now more than ever, that the chief priests and Pharisees are out to get Jesus, and thus have publicly denounced Him.

What the Fathers Say

"For the wedding garment is taken in honour of the union, that is, the union of the Bridegroom to the Bride. You know the Bridegroom; He is Christ. You know the Bride; it is the Church. Pay honour to the Bride, pay honour to the Bridegroom. If you pay due honour to them both, you will be their children. Therefore, make progress in this. Love the Lord, and so learn to love yourselves; that when, by loving the Lord you shall have loved yourselves, you may securely love your neighbour as yourselves."

- St Augustine

Liturgical

All hours of the Paschal services are prayed outside of the sanctuary except for the 1st hour of Holy Thursday and the 12th hour of Good Friday. Liturgies and other services where there is a raising of incense are not prayed from Monday to Wednesday. This commemorates the Jewish tradition of keeping the Lamb of the Passover for 3 days before it is slain.

To bring to mind the atrocities committed by Judas, as of the end of this evenings service, the church stops all forms of greeting to one another, neither does it kiss the gospel or icons in remembrance of the deceitful kiss of betrayal by Judas to our Lord.

Reflections

Christ invites each one of us to His feast in the liturgy and in the partaking of Holy Communion. Which of the three guests are you? Those who refused to go to the feast? Those who went without being ready? Or those who enjoyed the union with God in this Heavenly banquet?

WEDNESDAY

WEDNESDAY

In the Gospel of the first hour we enter into a discussion between the Pharisees and the chief priests. They are discussing what they should do to Jesus, should they arrest Him? Should they leave Him free? If they leave Him free, then everyone will believe Him and this will cause a stirring of the people to the point of riot. Thus, the Jewish leaders imagined this and thought, "If we leave Him free to preach then He will divide the people and the Romans will come and take away both our place and the nation."

As mentioned before, the nation of the Jews was occupied by Roman rule. However, the Romans did not rule over the Jewish spiritual life, and in fact they let them be. In spite of this, the Jews were warned that if any of their practices interfered with Roman law or civil calm, then they would rid Judaism from the nation, and would have full Roman law and religion imposed upon them. Thus, the Chief priests and Pharisees did not want to cause uproar by imprisoning Jesus.

Then one of the priests speaks out. It is here that we are introduced to Caiaphas, the high priest for the year. Caiaphas says that it is good for one man to die, than for the whole nation to fall in complete subjection to Rome. The section that brings to mind many questions is the following verse, "Now this he (Caiaphas) did not do by his own authority; but being high priest that year he prophesied that Jesus would die for the nation."- John 11:51

It is clear that Caiaphas is plotting against

Jesus. He is without a doubt going against Jesus. So how can what he said be prophecy? How can God speak through a man that is trying to destroy the Son of God? Doesn't the gift of prophecy come from God? The answer: Yes he did prophecy, yes he is going against Jesus, and yes the gift of prophecy comes from God, but God still respects the office of the high priest. The personal faults and evils of the office holder do not diminish the grace of the office itself. So Caiaphas is truly prophesying. Yet, while Caiaphas is speaking about the death of Christ saving the Jewish people from the full power of the Romans, God's meaning is that the death of Christ will save all people from the full power of sin and death.

THE BETRAYAL

Within the Gospel of the third and ninth hour holds the story of the betrayal of Jesus. This is arguably the most disturbing part of the entire Passion story. One of Jesus' closest friends, one whom He saw as His brother, betrays Him, even to death!

The church, from as early as the second century, teaches us to fast every Wednesday and Friday. Friday to commemorate His death, and Wednesday to commemorate His betrayal, the two most agonising moments in Jesus' life. In knowing the loving nature of Jesus, I am sure what would have hurt Him more than His death and physical sufferings, was His betrayal by Judas Iscariot.

What the Fathers Say

"Judas was chosen among the Twelve Apostles, and had charge of the money bag, to lay it out upon the poor, that it might not seem as though he had betrayed the Lord because he was not honoured or in need. Therefore the Lord granted him this office, that He might also be justified in him; he would be guilty of a greater fault, not as one driven to it by wrong done to him, but as one misusing grace."

– St Ambrose

Allow me to set the scene. The Pharisees have now had enough of Jesus. He was openly rebuking and verbally chastising the Jewish leaders. He was putting way too much negative attention on them! He had more fans and followers than any Pharisee! He performed miracles, signs, and wonders that none of them could even imagine doing! His teachings bluntly and justifiably rebuked even the greatest of Pharisees. No matter what they threw at Him, whatever questions, or trials, or tests, Jesus answered them all to shame! He conquered every trial and aced every test! No matter what the Pharisees and leaders tried to silence Jesus, it did not work! Thus they were fed up, and had enough. They no longer wanted Him around. They did not just want Him silenced, they wanted Him dead!

Enter Judas Iscariot. Judas, despite being a disciple of Jesus, lusted very much over money. He was greedy and his whole heart was not following the Lord, but it also followed much of the material world. Judas knew the Jews were desperate and would do anything to get rid of Jesus, so he dabbled with the devil, let Satan into his heart and lost himself. Judas heeded the call of the Jewish leaders and agreed in his heart to betray God. Truly Jesus was right when He said, "No one can serve two masters; for either he will hate the one and love the other, or else he will be loyal to the one and despise the other. You cannot serve God and mammon." – Matthew 6:24

You see, the whole time! The whole time throughout the three years of Jesus' ministry, when all the disciples were selected, someone was watching! The whole time, when they were working, someone was watching! When they ate, drank, slept, prayed, laughed, cried....Satan was watching! Waiting! Waiting for the right time to attack. He was watching and analysing waiting for the perfect time to destroy them all. So he looked at their hearts, their minds, and their souls and if they gave him the chance, he ventured in. You see, we know that God has a plan for our lives... but sometimes we allow satan to distroy this plan

Satan will come and go in our lives, and just because you can't see him, you assume he is not there, but Satan is there, watching, waiting for his chance to cause you to fall. And don't think for a second he is doing it because you're a threat. Who are you!?! Who are any of us!?! He would attack even the least of us in full knowledge that destroying us hurts God! The whole time Satan is attacking us he is looking up at God and wickedly smiling, thinking in his mind that God lost this one.

God's heart is more torn and hurt when we sin then any pain you could ever imagine. Nothing

What the Fathers Say

"Whoever it is, open for him and let him come in. If he is hungry, behold, in your house is the Bread of Life. If he is thirsty, behold, the Blessed Fountain is in your dwelling. If he is sick and asks for healing, behold, the Great Physician is here."

– St Ephraim the Syrian

hurts God more than our betrayal of Him. And every time we sin, that is exactly what we do. We betray Him. Judas let Satan in. Judas dropped his guard and performed the most painful thing known...he betrayed his Protector, his Provider, his Creator, his Friend, his Brother, his Father, his Master, his Everything... he betrayed his God!

Now the Bible tells us of the betrayal of Jesus in three verses. Yet, the betrayal was so much deeper than three verses. Throughout all of history, the most evil crime ever committed was the betrayal of Jesus Christ, and the most painful sin to God was the betrayal of Christ by Judas Iscariot!

People, Places and Things

Caiaphas

Caiaphas was promoted to the high priesthood around the year 18 AD. Caiaphas served as high priest at the time of Jesus' crucifixion and was the son-in-law of Annas, a former High Priest. He was a leader in the plot to end the life of Christ. He was the son-in-law of Annas, a former high priest, and in this way he inherited his position. His reign as high priest ended around the year 37 AD. Caiaphas is the one that prophesies that the death of Jesus would save the Jewish nation, despite his twisted understanding of it.

Purification

Purification is a Jewish ritual of cleansing. In order for anyone to participate in worship they are required to complete this rite first. The ritual consisted of three stages:

MARY ANOINTS THE HEAD OF JESUS

The church now decides to put what seems to be a strange Gospel for the sixth hour. It is a recount of the anointing of Jesus' feet by Mary, the sister of Lazarus and Martha. This story is put between both Gospel accounts that speak of the betrayal of Jesus by Judas. It is as though the church is providing for us a flash back of the event, but why?

The reason for this is the disciple that rebuked Mary for her great act of faith was Judas. In fact, throughout all four Gospel accounts, this is the only time Judas ever indicated any sort of evil thought. Judas says "Why was this fragrant oil not sold for three hundred denarii and given to

1. Stage one involved the use of water. The people were required to wash themselves and their clothes.

2. Stage two involved the use of blood. The blood was used to purify the holy places such as the altar.

3. Finally, the third stage involved the use of fire. The fire was required for the sacrifices that needed to be made in order to complete the right of

purification. Varying sacrifices were needed for various events. For example, after childbirth, the mother was required to purify herself by sacrificing a lamb and a pigeon or turtledove.

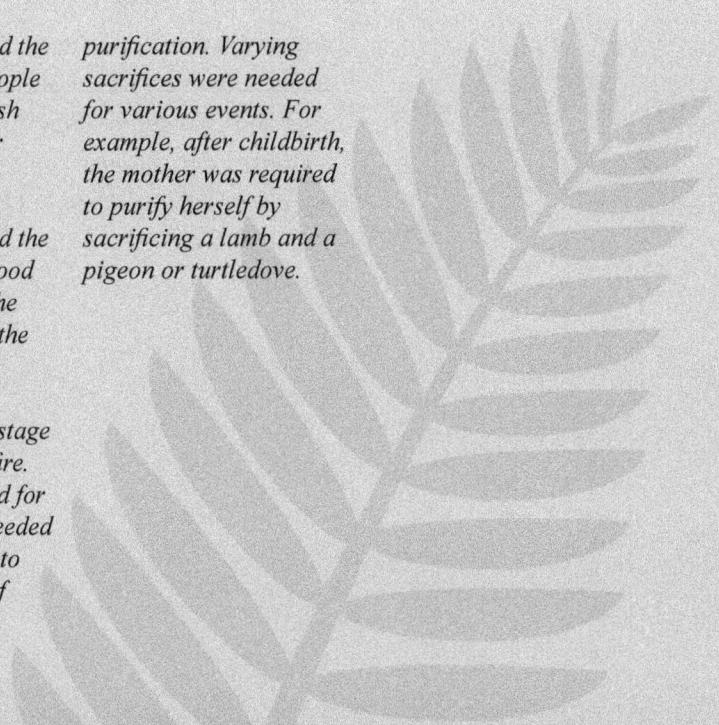

the poor?" They say sin is like a worm that lives inside us; the more we leave it, the more it eats at us and grows. It may very well be that it was at this point in time that the worm of sin began to show its head in Judas. It ate away at him, and all of a sudden, the things that proceeded from Jesus' mouth that once pleased Judas are now annoying and caused discomfort. Judas left the worm to grow inside of him and it began to eat away at him until it completely consumed him and he fell.

The church is very wise in its choosing of the readings for this day. At first glance, putting the story of when Mary of Bethany (the sister of Martha and Lazarus) anoints the head of Jesus (6th hour Gospel) in the middle of three accounts of Judas' betrayal of Jesus (1st 3rd and 9th hour Gospels) is a little strange. Nonetheless, after deeper observation we see that it is very relevant. The church is trying to show that, just as Mary of Bethany had an opportunity to repent, so also did Judas. Judas very well could have repented on the spot and changed his ways that were leading to his destruction, he even could have repented after he committed his crimes, but he didn't.

Thus the church is telling us not to be like Judas. Not that we must never sin again, because we are human and God knows that we are weak, but when God presents an opportunity to come to Him then we should take it with both hands. We should bow down before the feet of Christ with a repentant heart as Mary did, rather than harden our hearts and widen our conscience and ignore the messages from God as Judas did. Even after we sin we must turn back to God and repent, never losing hope and knowing very well that God will accept us, just as He did with Mary.

Liturgical

In terms of liturgical happenings, Wednesday is the exact same as the previous day. However, there is one special reading that is added to this day. During the 11th hour, a recount of the story of Job is read out. It is not the word for word account found in the bible, but gives a detailed explanation of the trials and tribulations faced by Job and his endurance through them. The idea is to contrast the sufferings of Job with the sufferings of Christ.

Reflections

Some of us have this one sin that we can never bring ourselves to mention in confession. Will you let it grow to destroy my life or will I RUN to confess it?

THURSDAY EVE

THURSDAY EVE

Thursday eve presents to us Christ as the Son of God. In all the Gospels except the 3rd hour Gospel, Jesus is continually referring to Himself as the Son of God. It is also said by the Fathers to be the "night of hearts". Throughout this night we will come across various characters with different hearts and attitudes toward God.

In the Gospel of the 1st hour, taken from St John's Gospel, Jesus once again tells of His upcoming death, but this time is a bit different. Instead of mentioning that He will be delivered, betrayed or lifted up, He mentions that no one is able to take His life, only when He decides to die will He die. This is very accurately seen at the 9th hour of Good Friday. When Christ was on the cross, He decided when it was time to die saying, "'It is finished!' and bowing His head, He gave up His spirit." – John 19:30. This verse clearly is a fulfilment of the words spoken of by Jesus in this 1st hour Gospel of Thursday eve. It is a statement highlighting the divinity of Jesus as the Christ, the only begotten Son of God. It is here that we see the sacrificial heart of Christ. Jesus, in trying to comfort His disciples of the upcoming events, tells His disciples that He is going to die, but it will be out of His own will and authority, and for their benefit. It is in the sacrificial heart of Christ to die for the salvation of the whole world, but this is once again rejected in the minds of the disciples.

MARY ANOINTS JESUS' HEAD (3ᴿᴰ HOUR)

The church, in the Gospel of the 3rd hour, according to St Mark, tries to contrast the heart of Mary of Bethany, with Judas Iscariot. Mary, who hadn't been anywhere near as close to Jesus as Judas was, had neither seen anywhere near as many miracles, nor heard Him speak as often, how was she so easily able to accept Christ, while Judas could not? During Judas' years as a disciple, he received many things from the Lord, yet his love for money, for the materialistic, and his lust for the world, failed him, while Mary knew Christ by the purity of her heart and the love that was inside of her. This is the loving heart.

It is in the Gospels of the 3rd and 6th hours that we see the frustration of Christ toward the unbelieving Jews. After years of unquestionable proofs, life changing miracles, and divine words, the Jews are still unbelieving. Perhaps many of them did believe, maybe some genuinely wanted more proof, maybe the raising of Lazarus from the dead after four days wasn't enough or the creation of a man's eyes wasn't enough, or feeding over five thousand people with five loaves and two fish wasn't enough, but if they weren't enough then what else would convince them?

What the Fathers Say

"They became blinded because of their disbelief in God. They look at Him, yet do not see Him; as to them, He is, as though, not there; as the case is with the sun — His creation — which blinds those with weak vision; to be unable to see its light. As to those who believe in Him and follow Him, He grants greater enlightenment to their minds."

- St Irenaeus

The Fathers believe that there was more than enough proof! And the only reason the Jews, in particular the elders, did not turn to Jesus is because their hearts were hardened. The Jewish elders knew the law and the prophets and should have recognised that Jesus was accomplishing all things, but they hardened their hearts, just as Pharaoh did with Moses. They were afraid that they would lose their status. They were afraid that if He was the Messiah, then all of what He said about them being hypocrites and them turning people away from God was true. It is however noted in the gospel of St John that there were certain Pharisees who did believe in Jesus "but they did not confess Him, lest they should be put out of the synagogue; for they loved the praise of men more than the praise of God"–John12:42-43.

People, Places and Things

Judas Iscariot

Judas Iscariot, the betrayer of Jesus. He is mentioned last in every account of the naming of the 12 due to his unrepentant betrayal of Jesus. Judas is the Greek name for Judah, while the word Iscariot is Aramaic for "man of Kerioth" which is a town not too far from Hebron, making Judas the only disciple from Judea.

Judas was the treasurer of funds for the disciples and is quoted in the bible as a thief of those funds.

High Priest

The high priest is the one who is in charge of Temple worship. He would be equivalent to a modern day Bishop or Patriarch. The high priest also has certain responsibilities to justly

We may criticise these Pharisees for choosing the praise of men over the praise of God, but can we honestly say that we don't do the same? When we see something wrong being done, how often would we stand up for what is right, even if it means that we will lose popularity with a certain group of friends for the sake of Christ? When your boss asks you if you can work on Sundays, do you say yes? When you are the only one of your friends that is fasting, do you break it just to fit in? Why are you embarrassed of what people are asking, when you have clearly been given a chance to testify for God! Why worry more about what people will think about you then what God, your Creator, your King, your biggest Fan and the One that loves you the most will think of you? The heart spoken of in this hour is the hardened heart. Jesus warns against this type of heart.

What the Fathers Say

"For He was not stripped of the flesh by obligation of any authority, but He stripped Himself...and so the Son of God lowered himself to become our friend in the fellowship of death."

- St Augustine

judge the Jews in civil matters. Orignally the position was one that lasted for the entire life of the position holder. However, during the Roman occupation, Roman officials chose the position of High priest. After this point the position was held for a maximum of 1 year. Josephus, a 1st century historian says that there were 4 High priests throughout the ministry of Christ, all descending from the lineage of Annas who was High Priest throughout Christs time but before His ministry began. Ishmael the son of Phabi was the first High Priest during Christs ministry, then Eleazer the son of Annas, followed by Simon son of Camithus and ending with Caiaphas who was the son-in-law of Annas.

Liturgical

This entire day and evening is liturgically dedicated to reminding us of the huge betrayal made by Judas to his Master and God. The idea is that we too bring to mind our own betrayals we have committed to our beloved Lord throughout the year, and that we repent from these atrocities.

The Psalm of the 3rd hour is of particular importance. It is in the same "shami" royal tune as "Pekethronos". The Psalm is called "Av etchinon" – Psalm 55:21 and translates to, "your words were softer than oil, yet they were drawn swords." The psalm is sung to highlight the deceptive person of Judas. Whilst his lips were singing and praising Christ, his heart was set on destroying the One that loved him with all His heart.

Reflections

If Jesus came to your room today, as He did to Mary, what would you change?

THURSDAY

Events

THURSDAY

WASHING OF THE FEET

Now in preparation for the Passover celebration, Jesus' disciples killed the Passover lamb and approached the Lord and asked Him where they were going to dine for the evening. Jesus told two of them to go into town; on the way they were to meet a man carrying a pitcher of water. He then instructed them to follow him and whichever house he enters, inform the master of that house that "the Teacher" has need of your guest room so He may eat the Passover with His disciples. So the disciples went and did as they were told and were led to a "large upper room, furnished, and prepared" in which they celebrated the Passover.

During the celebration Jesus becomes disturbed and troubled. When His disciples start to question Him He tells them, "One of you will betray Me." The disciples are shocked and are completely lost for words. All they can ask is, "is it I, is it I Lord?"

There was one resting on the chest of Jesus, John, known as John the Beloved and one of Christ's closest followers. Simon Peter seeing John resting on the Lord, gets John's attention and asks him to question the Lord on who will betray Him. John does so and asks the Lord. Jesus then replies and quietly tells John, "It is he to whom I shall give a piece of bread when I have dipped it." – John 13:26. The Master then dips a piece of bread and hands it to Judas Iscariot, who eats it and looks up to Jesus. Jesus looking back tells him, "What you do, do quickly." At that point the devil took over Judas's heart and he went to betray the Lord.

One of my favourite sections of all of Holy Week is what happens next. After they had eaten and celebrated the Passover, Judas having already left to betray Jesus, and Jesus knowing that all things were about to be fulfilled, gets up, takes off His outer garments, picks up a towel and wraps it around His waist. He then pours water into a basin and begins to wash His disciples' feet.

I doubt that we actually realise how incredible this moment in time really was, so allow me to put this in to a modern day context.

Let's say you go on a church camp, and your priest takes you on a bush walk, but not just any bush walk, a hard, gruelling journey that exhausts every fibre in your body; high mountains, steep slopes, small cave areas, large bush lands, and worst of all it has been raining the whole week,

What the Fathers Say

"Come then Lord Jesus, put off Your garments, which You put on for my sake; be stripped that You may clothe us with Your mercy. Gird Yourself for our sakes with a towel, that You may gird us with Your gift of immortality. Pour water into the basin, wash not only our feet but also the head, and not only the body, but also the footsteps of the soul. I wish to put off all the filth of our frailty, so that I also may say, "By night I have put off my coat, how shall I put it on? I have washed my feet, how shall I defile them?" How great is that excellence! As a servant, You wash the feet of Your disciples."

– St Ambrose

so every single time you take a step, you sink up to your knees in mud! An hour in to the walk you start to really work up a sweat and by the time you finish you are covered in mud, drenched in sweat and are so tired and sore that every muscle, ligament and fibre below your neck is numb. You finally finish the walk and return to the campsite and you all collapse on the floor. Every single one of you is absolutely starving, exhausted, and stink, but you are all way too tired to go and take a shower or to get up and go to bed, and just when you are about to totally give up and set up camp on the floor for the night, your priest, the head of your church and one of the most powerful and influential people in your life, without saying a word gets up, prepares food for everyone and then, beyond any comprehension, gets down on his hands and knees and washes the feet of every single one of you! The priest, despite having walked the same trip as you, despite being just as tired as you, and despite that he clearly has a much higher status and rank than you, has humbled himself and washed your stinky, muddy feet and for the sole purpose of his incredible love for you! The warmth that fills your body, that clear feeling of love that overflows from the priest's hands to your heart is overwhelming. How awesome is it that the hands which baptised you, or that give you Holy Communion, are the same hands that are washing you clean.

Now let's apply this to the disciples. The Lord, the Creator of heaven and earth, the One who controls the universe in the palms of His hands, has not only come down from His Holy Throne of Glory in heaven to our humility on earth, not only has He come down in the flesh and become incarnate of the Holy Spirit and of the holy virgin St Mary, not only has He come down in the flesh and preached to the world the true and full teachings of God and brought all those who would hear Him to the Father and has gathered us to Him, but He has come down, down to His very hands and knees and washed our stinky, muddy feet, the very feet of the human race who rejected Him in the beginning! He removed the stinky stench of sin! He removed the muddy stain of the fall of humanity! He removed the exhausting, fatigued, trapped feeling of separation from God! How beautiful it is to think that the hands that created your feet are the same hands that are cleaning it!

The fathers also interperted the washing of the feet as a symbol of confession. Jesus says that "He who is bathed needs only to wash his feet, but is completely clean." – John 13:10. Those who have been bathed are those who have been baptised. Thus those who are baptised only need to have confession to be clean in God's eyes. And in a deep desire for all to be clean in His eyes, He commands His disciples to "Go and do likewise!"

THE FIRST LITURGY

After He had washed His disciples' feet, He sat down with them to celebrate the first ever liturgy. The entire last supper story is one of the most intimate times between Jesus and His disciples. Not only does He share with them His

What the Fathers Say

"When we eat the holy body of Christ, the Saviour of us all, and drink of His precious blood, we thus obtain the life in us, for we become as if we are one with Him; we dwell in Him, and He too reigns in us. Do not doubt, for this is true, since He is the One who says it clearly"

– St Cyril the great

What the Fathers Say

"We thank God that when we were outside the city, carrying the shame of sin, the Lord opened the door of the Holy of Holies to us. He opens to us His holy altar and gives us His Holy Body and Holy Blood. It is a great blessing that the Lord remembered us during His week of suffering..."

– H.H. Pope Shenouda III

last meal before His death, not only does He wash their feet and their sins, but He also, for the first time, establishes the Mystery of Holy Communion.

Now it says in the Gospels that Jesus broke bread and prayed. Prayed? What did Jesus pray? Not many people know this, but Jesus prayed a prayer that all Jews pray before they eat the Passover. It is a prayer in Hebrew that is still prayed till today, and is translated as such:

"Blessed are You O Lord our God, King of the universe, who brings forth bread from the earth."

And here is a goose bump moment. In this prayer, Jesus foretells His death and Resurrection... through a prayer that Jews have been praying for thousands of years, in a section of the prayer that had an unknown double meaning that was overlooked for generations, and was never understood until that point in time. Remember, that throughout the ministry of Jesus, He taught, "I am the Bread of Life?" In saying this prayer, Jesus is prophesying that He would be broken and put to death and buried in the earth, in a tomb, and He, the Bread of life would be raised from the tomb of the earth and live again.

"Blessed are You O Lord our God, King of the universe, who brings forth bread from the earth."

The Jews had been praying this prayer every day and every night throughout their lives, and not even His disciples knew the meaning of this prayer beyond its face value. This is exactly the point that Jesus was speaking about in Matthew 6:7 when He says "and when you pray do not use vain repetitions..." Therefore, try your best to pay attention to what you and the church recite at the times of prayer and don't breeze through it. There is always a meaning or treasure that is always overlooked. Even if you pray something everyday, there is still something new to be learnt from it. Prayer is dynamic; one day a prayer will mean one thing, another day it will mean something else. God's message is alive and no matter what your situation, God has an answer for you.

People, Places and Things

Passover

The feast of Passover is the most important feast on the Jewish calendar. It is in commemoration of the salvation of the people of God from the bondage of slavery in Egypt. The lamb would be chosen on the 10th day of that month and would be slain and eaten four days later, on the 14th day of that month. This was symbolic of Christ, our lamb, who was slain for our salvation and released us from the slavery of sin.

Unleavened bread

Leaven is like yeast and causes the dough to rise. Unleavened bread is bread baked without the use of any yeast. The Passover is also called the feast of unleavened bread since only unleavened bread was consumed for the next seven days following the Passover. This was to commemorate the fact that the Israelites had no time to put leaven or yeast in their bread when they were set free from slavery and needed to flee Egypt.

WASH YOUR FEET BEFORE YOU EAT!

Notice how Jesus washed the feet of His disciples before He fed them the Holy Communion. Likewise we need to confess and repent before we partake of the Lord's Holy body and Sacred blood.

THE MAN WITH A PITCHER

Two of the Lord's disciples were told to go and find a man carrying a pitcher of water. Tradition tells us that man was the evangelist St Mark, thus making the house of St Mark the house of the first Holy Communion and liturgy and hence the first church.

Liturgically speaking, Thursday is a very busy day. The day begins in the sanctuary with the first hour being prayed with a raising of incense service. The raising of incense is performed for two reasons; firstly to highlight the readings of the day, as many readings refer to Old Testament sacrifices and raising of incense, and secondly, the liturgy is going to be celebrated later in the day, and it is necessary for a raising of incense service to be performed before the liturgy is celebrated.

Various hymns are sung during the first hour of this day. However, the most stand out is the chant "Judas". This is one of the strongest liturgical messages performed by the church. Whilst this chant is sung, the deacons in disgust at the betrayal, of Judas, perform a reverse procession around the church. In times of celebratory processions, the deacons would walk out of the altar and process around the church in an anti-clockwise motion. However, during this procession, as a sign of the churches rejection of Judas' acts, it processes around the church in a clockwise motion, with all participants walking backwards around the church once then return back to their places. All the instruments that are played are played inside out portraying the rejection of Judah's shameful act, and the tune of the chant itself evoke emotions of disgust and bitterness. The church then again chants the psalm "Avetchinon" – Psalm 55:21, as it did the previous night, to further highlight its rejection of the acts of Judas.

The 3rd, 6th and 9th hour prayers are all prayed outside the sanctuary again as the usual Paschal prayers, and all follow the exact same structure of Paschal service as the other days.

At the conclusion of the 9th hour the priest and deacons all change into their liturgical vestments and begin the liturgy of the blessing of the water (Lakan). The service involves many litanies and prayers for both those in the church and the whole world. The entire service is prayed in the annual tune and is not in the sad mournful tune. After the blessing of the water is completed the gospel is read. It is the reading of when Christ washes the feet of His disciples. You will notice that at the point when the deacon reads concerning Jesus, "rose from supper and laid aside His garments, took a towel and girded Himself." The priest will likewise take a towel or a long piece of material and gird his waist, with it he will wet the tip in the water that was just prayed on and will do the sign of the cross on the feet of the entire congregation present. The idea of this liturgy is to wash the feet of the congregation who are the Disciples of Christ, as Jesus washed the feet of His 12 disciples and said, "go do likewise".

After the completion of the liturgy of the blessing of the water, the veil of the sanctuary is opened and the priest and deacons ascend to the altar to begin the liturgy in commemoration of the first celebration of the liturgy by Christ with His disciples at the last supper, which takes place on this day. The liturgy is prayed in the annual tune, however various sections that refer to Christ's death, resurrection and ascension are skipped as given we are in passion week, we have not reached the death or resurrection or ascension of Christ yet.

For example, the readings of the Catholicon epistle as well as the Acts and the synaxarion are not read.

During the distribution of the Holy Communion, Psalm 150 should not be prayed, but instead, the church begins the prayers of the 11th. Since the distribution of the Holy Body and Sacred blood of Christ is taking place, the whole church should be standing throughout all the readings, even though it would usually be permitted to sit during these times.

FRIDAY EVE

Events

FRIDAY EVE

In the readings of the First hour of Friday eve, Jesus embarks on one of the most beautiful and loving sermons ever. This sermon, John chapters 13 – 17, is known as the "Farewell Discourse". It is also known as the "Paraclete" or "Comforter" chapters, as Jesus speaks of the promise of the Holy Spirit the Paraclete, and for its incredible ability to provide comfort to the reader.

To go through and analyse all the chapters of the "Farewell Discourse", with focus on each verse would take a lifetime. Instead lets take a look at a one of the most important and beautiful verses in this passage.

"A new commandment I give to you, love one another; as I have loved you, that you also love one another."

As beautiful as this command is, to some, it seems to be a contradiction. Jesus speaks of a new commandment, but loving one another is not a new commandment at all? When Jesus was approached by the lawyer in Luke chapter 10, the lawyer asks Him, "What shall I do to inherit eternal life?" so Jesus says, "What is written in the law? What is your understanding of it?" the lawyer then replies, " 'You shall love the LORD your God with all your heart, with all your soul, with all your strength, and with all your mind' and ' your neighbour as yourself.' " To which Jesus responds, "You have answered rightly; do this and you will live."

Wait a minute... if loving one another is a new commandment then how was the lawyer correct in his answer? How could it possibly have been in the Law? Did Jesus make a mistake? No! Not at all! The key difference is in what manner we ought to love one another... "Love one another, AS I HAVE LOVED YOU."

These words, "as I have loved you," add a whole new dimension to love. When Jesus was abandoned He still loved those who abandoned Him, when Jesus was reviled He still loved those who were reviling Him. When He was mocked and yelled at, falsely accused, wrongfully judged, betrayed, beaten, spat on, whipped, even whilst He was crucified He still loved those who were doing wrong to Him. Loving those who love you is easy, "For even the sinners love those who love them" but to love your enemies, and to do good to those who hate you....that is something completely unheard of.

So while the commandment to love one another always existed, the command to love one another with the same measure by which Jesus loved is an entirely foreign and new concept.

AT GETHSEMANE (3ᴿᴰ AND 6ᵀᴴ HOURS)

As the final hours of Jesus' life approached, after He had finished with His disciples, He went to the garden of Gethsemane. Christ would often retreat with His disciples to this garden for prayer.

Once Jesus gets to the garden He tells His

What the Fathers Say

"His whole heart was deeply with others. He had two matters in mind: How to save the world, and how to keep His disciples safe from tribulation."

– H.H. Pope Shenouda III

disciples to stay and wait while He took Peter, James and John, and journeyed further into the garden, where "He began to be sorrowful and deeply distressed." He says to them, "My soul is exceedingly sorrowful, even to death." He then asks them to stay in a certain place and to "watch." Jesus withdrew from them; only a stone throw away, i.e. a short distance, then, out of the absolute overwhelming sorrow He was feeling, collapses and bowing Himself down He begins to pray. Looking up to His Father He reasons and says "O My Father, if it is possible, let this cup pass from Me; nevertheless, not as I will, but as You will." After He had prayed Jesus goes to see His disciples to check on them and perhaps find some comfort. He finds them asleep. He turns to Peter and says, "Could you not watch with Me one hour? Watch and pray, lest you enter into temptation. The spirit indeed is willing but the flesh is weak." Jesus for a second time leaves the three disciples to go back and pray, and again reasons with the Father, "O My Father, if this cup cannot pass away from Me unless I drink it, Your will be done." Again Jesus, after He has prayed returns to Peter, James and John, and again for the second time finds them asleep. Jesus again returns and prays the same words more earnestly. Then according to the gospel of St Luke, "an angel appeared to Him from heaven, strengthening Him." The sorrow and emotional torment of the painstaking nightmare of carrying the sins of the world took a huge emotional toll on Jesus, which translated to a physical phenomenon that caused Him to sweat "great drops of blood." Finally Jesus had concluded His prayer, and for the third time He found His disciples "sleeping and resting," yet this time He tells them not only to pray, but to "rise and pray"-Luke 22:46 because it was approaching the end and "the Son of Man is being betrayed into the hands of sinners." - Mark 14:41

THE SEIZING OF CHRIST (9TH HOUR)

Before Christ had even finished what He was saying, Judas Iscariot, one of Jesus' disciples, approached the garden with a "great multitude with swords and clubs." As the multitude loomed they wondered where they would find Jesus, so the Lord, in all bravery, asks them, "Whom are you seeking?" to which they reply, "Jesus of Nazareth" and to their shock and astonishment the Lord tells them, "I am He." The troops were clearly not expecting to hear that. The Jewish elders made Jesus out to be a tyrant and a leader of a group of rebels, thus the troops had prepared themselves for a battle and Jesus' response would have been shock enough but I am sure that they must have heard some rumours of Jesus being the Messiah and in that instant they must have suspected that claim to be true and felt power come forth from His mouth when He says "I am He" to the extent that they fell to the ground in disarray and were taken back by what had just happened. Thus their confusion prompted Jesus to ask them again, "Whom are you seeking?" and they said "Jesus of Nazareth." Jesus answered, "I have told you I am He. Therefore, if you seek Me, let these (the disciples) go there way." '

What the Fathers Say

"Therefore, there is no farewell between you and Me because there is no separation at all. How beautiful is this comparison with all this love, passion and comfort at a time like this. Blessed are You Lord in all Your great comfort."

- H.H. Pope Shenouda III

Whilst the troops were still in utter disarray as to why their so called righteous religious leaders want to condemn such a seemingly peaceful man, they remembered that before the encounter took place, Judas had given the troops a sign so they would know whom to arrest. "Whomever I kiss, He is the One, seize Him." - Matt 26:48 So Judas approached Christ, he greeted Him and kissed Him. Despite knowing exactly why Judas was there, and exactly what he was doing, the Lord in all His loving ways still kissed Judas and partook of Judas' greeting, and instead of condemning Judas, the Lord says to him, "Judas My friend, why have you come? Are you betraying the Son of Man with a kiss? A symbol of love?"

As the Lord was speaking to Judas, Jesus' disciples put all the pieces together and finally made full sense of what was happening: Judas had just betrayed Jesus his Christ, and the multitude of men with weapons were there to escort Jesus

People, Places and Things

Gethsemane

Gethsemane is a garden east of Jerusalem, on the Mount of Olives. Gethsemane was most likely a closed off garden, perfect for Jesus and His disciples to pray, rest, and be in fellowship with each other. The word Gethsemane is translated to "olive press".

Sanhedrin

The Sanhedrin is the first century high council of the Jews, headed by a high priest. It is made up of 71 members that were mostly Sadducees and the rest were Pharisees. Moses began the Sanhedrin in the book of Numbers 11:16, however, the Sanhedrin in the time of Moses had a fairly different role.

to the authorities. So, they asked Jesus whether or not to attack the men and protect Him, and before they heard a response, Simon Peter pulled out a sword and cut off the ear of one of the men, Malchus, who was a servant of the high priest.

Whether or not Peter's actions were a result of bravery or absurdity is up for debate, but whatever the reason, Jesus was not happy with it, and rebukes Peter. He reminds Peter that He needs to drink the cup His Father has given Him, and teaches that he who lives by the sword, will die by the sword. He further reminds Peter that if this were the way He was to deal with violence He could simply ask His Father, and He would send Him more than twelve legions of angels.

Then a beautiful thing happens. Jesus in all humility yet with total authority, showing that He truly is both all-powerful and all-loving, picks up the severed ear of the man there to arrest Him, and heals him, thus reattaching Malchus' severed ear.

What the Fathers Say

"This love in His heart towards them (disciples) encourages us. He reminds us that we are not alone, but He is with us all our days until the end of the age."

– H.H. Pope Shenouda III

Sadducees

The Sadducees are a Jewish political party, and quite influential during the time of Jesus. They occupied a large proportion of the Sanhedrin. It is believed that Caiaphas was a Sadducee. Just as with the Pharisees, the Sadducees were formed at the time of the Maccabees around the year 200 B.C. It is believed they descended from an Old Testament priest by the name of Zadok, who served at the time of king David. The name Sadducees means "righteous ones". Sadducees are commonly known in the New Testament as not believing in the resurrection of the dead and life after death.

Jesus then looks to the multitude and questions them as to why they have come so heavily armed and in such great number, as if they were to arrest a criminal, or some kind of rebel leader. Jesus said that everyday He was present and teaching in the temple, and they could have seized Him then in front of the people, so why didn't they seize Him then? He said this to highlight the corruptness and secrecy of the entire ordeal.

The troops then arrest Jesus and lead Him away. Respecting Jesus' request, the troops left the disciples who were with Him alone, yet from a distance Peter was following and saw Jesus was being led to the house of the high priest, where the Jewish leaders were all awaiting to condemn the Lord.

THE TRIALS BEGIN (11ᵀᴴ HOUR)

The Gospel of St John mentions that St John the Beloved and disciple of Jesus Christ was known to the high priest and thus was allowed

Reflections

Do you have a friend who betrayed you or used you? To what extent can you forgive and love him?

to enter the courtyard. Looking back, he saw St Peter standing outside the closed gates and John spoke to the servant girl who was the gate keeper and brought Peter in. As Peter was making his way to John, the gatekeeper asked St Peter, "You are not also one of His disciples, are you?" but Peter denied it and replied, "I am not!" and just like that, Peter denies his Lord.

It is interesting to note from this scenario that St John was clearly known to be an apostle of Jesus. There is no way the high priest would have known John and not known that he was a disciple of Jesus, since all St John did for the last three years was follow Jesus. Also, the gatekeeper asks St Peter whether or not he was "also" a disciple, which may imply that she knew St John was also a follower. It is also most likely that St John was present and heard the conversation between Peter and the gatekeeper, and thus Peter's first denial of the Lord. So despite the fact that Peter was aware all who were present knew John was a disciple of Jesus, Peter still denied being a follower of Christ, making his denial that much worse.

The night was very cold and glum, and so Peter went and warmed himself around a fire with some of the servants and officers, and as he warmed himself, another servant girl, who also was a gate keeper, probes Peter in front of all those warming themselves, "This is one of them,"- Mark14:69, "This fellow also was with Jesus of Nazareth." - Matt26:71. Peter denies it saying, "I am not!"

What the Fathers Say

"If you walked on water my brethren and you didn't fall, know very well that the Lord was holding your hands very tightly. So keep these hands with you, and watch and do not depend on yourself so you don't fall. Those who depend on their own strength and their power (like Peter) need to transform these feelings into prayer."

– H.H. Pope Shenouda III

Now the eleventh hour Gospel sets the scene for a very tense and frustrating trial. While Peter was outside denying Christ, Jesus was in a room surrounded by hating Jewish leaders who fully intended to have Him killed and accordingly created an illegitimate court to judge Him for His apparent "crimes." But before they took Jesus to Caiaphas the high priest, they sent Him first to Annas, his father-in-law. A corrupt and hell-bent council then begins to examine the pure Lord Jesus, with Annas asking Him about His teachings and His followers, not that he may learn from what Christ has to say, but that he may scrutinise and condemn Him. The Lord wisely replies to Annas and the council saying, "I spoke openly to the world. I always taught in synagogues and in the temple, where the Jews always meet, and in secret I have said nothing. Why do you ask Me?

People,
Places
and
Things

Annas

Annas was a priest around the time John the Baptist began his ministry. Governor Quirinious, governor of Syria in about 6 A.D, appointed him to the high priesthood. However, another ruler named Gratus in the year 15 A.D deposed Annas.

Despite this, Annas still held much power and was very influential among the Jews. He was still seen as an equal to the high priest, since the high priesthood was for life, and was a hereditary rank, and thus, while Annas was not the practising high priest he is still acknowledged as power behind his familial successor, Caiaphas, receiving the high priesthood, and was often still referred to as the high priest.

Ask those who heard Me what I said to them. Indeed they know what I said."

Then one of the officers who were present and heard the Lord's response was enraged and with unrighteous zeal, strikes Jesus accusing Him of speaking inappropriately to the high priest. Jesus then, in all compassion, looks at the officer and speaks, "If I have spoken evil, bear witness of this evil; but if well, why do you strike Me?" See how the Lord of all Creation is able to humble Himself when struck by His creation, and we are not even able to accept any insult to our ego. Unhappy with the progress of the meeting, Annas sends Jesus bound to Caiaphas who was also high priest.

Thus, when Jesus was arrested He was first taken to Annas, then to Caiaphas. Annas is also the one who questioned Peter, after Pentecost, in Acts chapter 4. The name Annas means "merciful".

Chief Priests

Chief priests were the leaders of the priests. The priests were those responsible for the sacrifices and offerings in holy places. At the time of Jesus, their duties were performed in the temple. The priests were very respected people, thus the chief priests were given much honour, and were seen as the peoples link to God.

Jesus reaches Caiaphas, and upon arrival, the council get straight back to trying to condemn Jesus to death. Many false witnesses were brought forth, but all their testimonies contradicted each other and those that did make sense were not reason enough to punish the Lord. In all that He was accused, Jesus "kept silent and answered nothing." It was absolute chaos! All were screaming and shouting allegations and condemnations. Until finally, Caiaphas, in dramatic fashion, rises from his chair, approaches Jesus and asks Him, "Are You the Christ, the Son of the Blessed?" Utter silence filled the room. You could feel the tension.

Jesus then looks straight through Caiaphas and as though He was looking at his soul says, "I am. And you will see the Son of Man sitting at the right hand of Power, and coming on the clouds of heaven." Then to add force to the accusation and to aggravate what He said, the high priest tore his clothes and cried out, "He has spoken blasphemy! What further need do we have of witnesses?"

Even though the tearing of clothes was a custom for Jews when they heard blasphemy, when Caiaphas tore his robes, he had fully rejected God. It symbolises that the Jews had now lost the glory of the priesthood, and that seat of the high priest was now vacant. Thus Jesus acted as the high priest when he presided over His own sacrifice on the cross for indeed Jesus is the true High Priest.

As Jesus was taken from Annas to Caiaphas, another, a relative of Malchus, the one who Peter cut off his ear, approaches Peter and accuses him of being a follower of Jesus questioning, "Did I not see you in the garden with Him?" Peter then exclaims "Man, I do not know what you are saying!" then immediately a rooster crowed, "And the Lord turned and looked at Peter," and with the interlocked eye contact, Peter remembered the words of Jesus concerning his denial of Him.

Truly Peter feels the full extent of his denial of the Lord and begins to weep "bitterly".

CONTRADICTION BETWEEN THE GOSPEL ACCOUNTS?

At times in the Gospels, there seems to be certain contradictions and differing facts between the different accounts. This leads some people to say that Christianity must therefore be a lie if even the Gospel writers have differing stories.

However, any truly rational and educated person can see there is no contradiction in any of the accounts, just different perspectives. Just as one person may claim to see an apple on a table, another may claim to see a table with an apple on it. In a court of law, if two or more witnesses have the exact same account of the crime that took place, then the judge and jury would dismiss the witnesses as false, and that they had colluded and discussed what they would say at the witness stand.

THE SECOND EDEN AND THE SECOND ADAM...

In the first garden, Eden, the first Adam fell due to disobedience to God, but in the second garden, Gethsemane, the second Adam, Jesus Christ, is comforted by angels as His will is in full submission to that of the Father's.

Friday eve is slightly different from the rest of the Paschal services. The previous services all contained one Gospel reading per hour, however, from Friday eve until the end of Good Friday, four Gospel readings are read each Paschal hour.

Liturgical

The 1st hour of this evening contains the four chapters of the Paraclete or Final Discourse readings, in which Jesus goes on to give His final and some of His most beautiful teachings ever. It is here also that He promises His disciples the gift of the Holy Spirit.

Also, from the 1st hour of this evening, the final extension to "thok te ti gom", "Ta gom…" which translates to, "My strength and my praise is the Lord who became my holy salvation" is added. This is done to highlight the incredible passion that is about to take place and to bring to mind that it is our Lord and God who will be suffering for our salvation.

Reflections

Do you sometimes manipulate or take out of context the words of Jesus in order to get what you want?

FRIDAY

Events

Friday 1st hour

In the early morning, after Caiaphas' dramatic display of dissatisfaction at the words of Jesus, the council spoke among themselves and decided to have the Lord killed. So they bound Him and sent Him to the Praetorium, to Pontius Pilate, the Roman governor and procurator.

When Judas saw this, and realized that Jesus had been condemned, he was "remorseful" and returned to the chief priests and elders and tried to give back the thirty pieces of silver with which he was paid to betray the Lord. But they acknowledged it as being blood money and ironically would not accept it back as that would be a sin. Yet somehow, their consciences was fine with plotting to murder the Lord. So Judas, in unreserved distress, threw the money at their feet, ran out and feeling the heaviness of his sin, falsely

People, Places and Things

The Potter's Field

The Potter's field is located just outside Jerusalem in a valley called "Hinnom." It is the area of land the chief priests, elders and those who conspired against Jesus bought with the money that Judas returned to them after he regretted betraying the Lord. The Jews refused to accept the money back from Judas because they realised that it was blood money, and it was used to betray someone to death. The field is used to bury those who die while on pilgrimage to Jerusalem. And thus for these reasons, it became known as the field of blood.

Praetorium

The emperor's palace is often referred to as the Praetorium. The Praetorium is also the place where the thinking that Jesus would not accept him back, gave up hope and went out and hung himself.

Therefore Jesus was taken to the Praetorium, however the Jews did not accompany Him inside, but only to the entrance, for if they had entered the Praetorium they would have defiled themselves and not been able to partake of the upcoming Passover celebrations.

So as the Jews were presenting Jesus to Pilate at the gate, they began to accuse the Lord of many trivial and petty things falsely saying, "He is against Caesar because He refuses to pay taxes and calls Himself a king, but we only have one king, that is Caesar." Pilate then turns to Jesus and is astonished that He is not defending Himself and that He remains silent. Pilate speaks to Jesus

governor would generally reside. The Praetorium is most often a former barracks of a Roman squadron, as was the case of Pontius Pilates' Praetorium.

Pontius Pilate

Pontius Pilate was the roman governor, also known as "procurator" or "prefect", of Judea. Educated estimates place Pilates' promotion to

power to be around 26 AD. History books tell us that Pilate was a fairly ruthless man, and would often aggravate the Jewish people with his anti-Jewish antics. He was the governor who presided over the trial of Jesus, and sentenced Him to be handed to the will of the Jews, and allowed the Lord to be crucified. Pilate was relieved of his duties as governor, not long after the crucifixion of Christ,

due to an incident where he disturbed the peace of the Samaritans by executing many of them as they observed their worship.

What the Fathers Say

"A lamb, He is silent yet He is the "Word" proclaimed by the "voice of one crying out in the wilderness". He is weakened, wounded; yet He cures every disease and every weakness. He is brought up to the tree and nailed to it, yet by the Tree of Life He restores us."

- St Gregory of Nazianzen

and asks, "Are You the king of the Jews?" Jesus answers him saying, "It is as you say." Yet even Pilate, despite his history of rash decisions can see that condemning a Man over believing He is a king is beyond unreasonable, for all Pilate knew, Jesus could have just been sick and delusional. So the governor explained to the Jews that he finds no fault in Jesus. The elders and those opposing Christ then began to be riled and spoke saying, "He stirs up the people, teaching throughout all Judea, beginning from Galilee." It was clear that Pilate did not want anything to do with the situation. It was also very clear that to Pilate the Jews had delivered Jesus out of sheer jealousy. Thus, when he heard Galilee, he asked if Jesus were a Galilean, and when He discovered the Lord was from Galilee, and thus Herod's jurisdiction, he sent Christ to Herod.

Accordingly, the Jews took Jesus to Herod, who was in Jerusalem for the upcoming Passover celebrations, more for political appearances than because of his faithfulness, as Herod was Arab in origin. When Herod laid his eyes on Jesus he was glad because he had heard many things about Him and really wanted to witness a miracle of some kind, thinking the Lord was some kind of sorcerer and entertainer. This is the same Herod, to whom it was said, wanted to kill Jesus in Luke chapter 13. Jesus courageously replied to these words by calling Herod a "fox." Consequently their meeting was bound to be a fascinating one. However, when Jesus' case was presented before Herod, even when given the opportunity, Jesus again did not open His mouth.

This annoyed Herod. Herod thought himself to be some kind of god, and believed whatever he said goes. However, Jesus completely shamed this thought. The Lord was not afraid of Herod in the slightest! Ultimately, no matter what accusation was brought before Herod concerning Jesus, they were all seen as void and invalid. After many attempts to aggravate Jesus, Herod reverts to animal ways and with his men of war, Herod treats Jesus, the King of kings, with "contempt and mocked Him, arrayed Him in a gorgeous robe, and sent Him back to Pilate."

What the Fathers Say

"He was silent, and quietly endured everything... to teach us all meekness and longsuffering. Let us now imitate Him"

- St John Chrysostom

Reflections

We always make mistakes, "for all have sinned and fallen short of the glory of God", but do we repent as St Peter did or do we doubt the compassionate forgiving love of God and give up all hope as Judas did?

Events

Friday 3rd hour

The Jewish authorities return Jesus to the Praetorium and await the governor. Pilate enters the Praetorium and calls Jesus to him and speaks again saying, "Are you the king of the Jews?" Jesus then lifts His head to Pilate and a very interesting conversation takes place:

Jesus: "Are you speaking for yourself about this, or did others tell you this concerning Me?"

Pilate: "Am I a Jew? Your own nation and the chief priests have delivered You to me. What have You done?"

Jesus: "My kingdom is not of this world. If My kingdom were of this world, My servants would fight, so that I should not be delivered to the Jews; but now My kingdom is not from here."

Pilate: "Are you the king of the Jews?

Jesus: "You say rightly that I am the king. For this cause I was born, and for this cause I have come into the world, that I should bear witness to the truth. Everyone who is of the truth hears My voice."

Pilate then, in a somewhat enlightened yet contemplative way, looks at the Lord and replies, "What is truth?" Pilate then walks out to the Jews and informs them that neither he nor Herod found anything to fault Jesus for. Hearing this, the Jews begin to feel as though their plan of murdering Jesus is falling apart, so they begin to fear that Jesus will be released and He and His followers may perhaps rebel against them. However, as their frustration boiled over, the governor offers them an alternative. Pilate reminds them that every feast "he was accustomed to releasing one prisoner to them." So, in the hope that they choose to release Jesus, Pilate asks the people if they would rather release Jesus "the King of the Jews?" or a rebel leader named Barabbas, who was jailed for murder and treason. This was a scheme from Pilate to try and show the Jews the difference between Jesus and a man who was really guilty of breaking the law and disturbing the peace. But the proud and arrogant chief priests and elders, seeing their opportunity, took it and began to persuade the multitudes to free Barabbas and "destroy Jesus." Then, as Pilate asks whom they wanted to free, the multitudes begin to repeatedly cry out, "Barabbas!"

Pilate perhaps thought that the people where crying out "Barabbas" because they misunderstood what the governor was saying, thus he asked them again, "What do you want me to do with Him whom you call the King of the Jews?"

As this was taking place, Pilate receives a message concerning Jesus from his wife's servant informing him that his wife "suffered many things today in a dream because of Him" and that she wants him to "have nothing to do with that just Man." Pilate now had a decision to make. Listen to Herod, his wife, and his own heart and free the innocent Man Jesus, or keep the peace between the Jewish nation and his government and convict the innocent Lord of all. Throughout history, leaders and politicians have made many bad decisions to please people, yet none was more catastrophic than this. Pilate heeds to the people,

What the Fathers Say

"His love towards us reaches its peak when He offered and sacrificed Himself, when He gave His life for ransom for many for the redemption of sins."

– H.H. Pope Shenouda III

releases Barabbas then asks, "What then shall I do with Jesus who is called Christ?"

Ruthlessly the crowds shouted, "crucify Him!" Surprised at their request, Pilate tries to appease them and releases to them Barabbas. So Pilate again asks them what they want done with the Lord, and to his surprise, the crowds again cried out, "crucify Him." Yet Pilate still wishing to rescue Jesus, tells them that Jesus does not deserve death and he will, "chastise Him and release Him."

We face very similar dilemmas every day. The basic dilemma of doing what is right, as opposed to doing what is easy. Doing what is right is hardly ever the easy option, and this was the case with Pilate. He had a decision to make, follow what he clearly seemed to know was right, or to take the easy way out, cave to the Jews request, and crucify Jesus. Every time we have the choice of doing something wrong, we face the exact same dilemma Pilate faced, we may even try and compromise so that we are only "partially wrong" just as Pilate did by scourging Christ. So we cannot be quick to judge, because we so often choose the ease of the world over the complex yet simple beauty of the ways of God.

As mentioned, Pilate is notoriously known for his harsh punishments, so although it is fairly clear that Pilate is trying to help Jesus, he still chastises Him in the traditional barbaric Roman way.

It doesn't seem fair that our most beloved and blameless Lord should have His back torn

What the Fathers Say

"For me, my Lord, You did not hide Your face from the shame of spitting... You came to slaughtering like a lamb, even to the cross..."

- The liturgy of St Gregory

off for no reason, but what in the entire Passion story is fair? Yet Christ still endures till the end! How often do we fall into situations that are very overwhelming, sometimes we may be at fault, other times we may be innocent, yet in all situations we complain and whine that it is unfair and refuse to see any good out of our circumstance. Christ very well could have done the same because He was entirely innocent, yet throughout it all, "He opened not His mouth." Sometimes we just need to stop complaining about our circumstances and remember what Christ went through, and if He had complained, then we would never have been saved. For your sake He opened not His mouth, so for His sake let's not open ours.

So the soldiers led the Lord away to the Praetorium and whipped Him with some of the most inhumane lashes ever known to man. They then began to beat Him and mock Him, they clothed Him in a purple robe, twisted on His precious head an insulting crown of thorns, and began to mockingly salute and bow to Him saying, "Hail, King of the Jews!" They then struck Him on the head with a reed and in a most disgusting fashion they spat on Him. The Creator was spat on, beaten and rejected by His creation.

Then once again Jesus was taken to Pilate in front of all the Jews. Pilate says to the multitudes, "Behold the Man!" and at this they all erupted and cried out as loud as they could and with a heart full of hatred, "Crucify Him, crucify Him!" They warned that if Pilate did not crucify Him then He was encouraging an enemy of Caesar.

What the Fathers Say

"He went away carrying His Cross… What a great scene – The King carrying the tree of punishment instead of the rod of a king. He carried the cross upon His shoulders like a shining candle instead of putting it under a bushel."

– St Augustine

Pilate, shocked at what he is hearing, cannot believe that a group of so called peaceful religious men and women would go to such lengths to have Jesus killed. The Jews would rather free a murderer than an innocent man than risk their pride and stature being dented. Further, not only did they want Him dead, but completely exterminated, tortured and crucified as if Jesus were the worst of all criminals.

Thus, in one final attempt to save Jesus, Pilate took Jesus privately and said to Him, "Where are you from?" But Jesus gave no answer. Then Pilate in frustration says, "Are you not speaking to Me? Do You not know that I have the power to crucify You, and to release You?" But to this the Lord replied, in all wisdom, showing us that wisdom is needed at all times even to the point of death,

People, Places and Things

Barabbas

Barabbas was a murderer and insurrectionist, a rebel leader and was seen as a criminal in the eyes of both the Jews and the Romans. He was caught and put in jail under the governance of Pontius Pilate. Barabbas is the one the Jewish leaders asked to release rather than Jesus. Barabbas means "son of the father." Various ancient writings, including ancient versions of the New Testament as well as a number of Greek manuscripts have Pilate calling Barabbas, 'Jesus Barabbas'.

Roman whipping

Whipping has been a very common form of punishment throughout history and is also referred to as scourging,

"You could have no power at all against Me unless it had been given you from above. Therefore the one who delivered Me to you has the greater sin." At these words Pilate was desperate to release Jesus, but he was backed into a corner by the Jews, for not only did they insist that freedom of Jesus meant betraying Caesar, but it was clear if he had released the Lord then there would be a riot. So in order to try and keep the peace, he took water and washed his hands before the multitude and said, "I am innocent of the blood of this just person. You see to it." The people answered, "His blood be on us and on our children." Sadly, these words have sure proven to be destructive for the Jewish people since then.

And just like that, they went to crucify Jesus.

flogging and flagellation. Roman whipping seemed however to be the most fierce. The whip consisted of various strands that had pieces of metal and bone attached to its tips that would cause serious trauma. It would often result in losses of large chunks of flesh and even removal of eyes. Whipping in the roman tradition was often reserved for non-roman citizens and would often leave them in hypovolemic shock, which causes the body to go into shock due to a large loss of blood. The whipping was designed to leave the victim "half dead" but was commonly found to completely kill. Many say that Jesus was whipped 39 times, because Jewish Law dictates that when they are whipped they should be lashed 40 times however in order to remove the risk of breaking the law due to a miscount, they would stop at 39. However, that was Jewish law, not Roman. Romans would often not even reach 39 lashes before the victim, who was chained to a pillar, was at the brink of death.

How easy is it to look at what they did to Jesus and judge them, but forget that we too are guilty of this everyday! Everyday we are confronted with battles, and the choices that we make are what determine the outcome of these battles. Battles of whether to wake up on Sunday because we are tired, but over the last 48 hours, Christ didn't even rest His eyes once. Battles of whether to fast or not, this whole day Christ neither ate nor drank a single thing. Battles of whether to go to a party that will lead to temptation and potential sin, or to stay up late chatting on the internet or over the phone to a boy or girl we may be attracted to even though we have been advised against it, battles of whether or not to gossip or to watch pornography, or to drink alcohol or to not forgive or to be violent or abusive. Each time we make a bad choice, willingly knowing that we are doing wrong, then it is as if we are with those shouting "Crucify Him, Crucify Him" because clearly we are rejecting Christ, and what God has taught us either through the Bible or through His church, means nothing to us. How easy it is to forget that each time we sin, we forget that Christ went up to the mount of Calvary, to be crucified as a common thief.

Of course at times it may not be easy, but every time you feel as though you are struggling and about to fall from the weight of your cross, do as Simon of Cyrene did: just look over your shoulder and look at the beautiful face of your ever-loving Creator who is carrying your cross with you.

Friday is by far the most action packed day on the churches liturgical calendar.

1st and 3rd hours – with the exception of a Pauline epistle being read after the prophecies, the priest raising incense before the Pauline, and the reading of the four Gospels from Friday eve onward, the 1st and 3rd hours are more or less the same as all other Paschal service hours.

The Paschal service of Good Friday takes a whole new leap forward from the already beautiful services of the previous days. The church is further decorated with flowers, with the centre piece that was originally at the front of the church at the steps of the Sanctuary replaced by a more beautiful and extravagant centre piece, decked out with flowers, lights, candles and many will also have a crown of thorns. This serves as a type of shrine to Christ and as a remembrance of what He experienced.

Reflections

It doesn't seem fair that our most beloved and blameless Lord should have His back torn off for no reason; but what in the entire Passion story is fair?

Events

Friday
6th hour

After the order was issued to crucify Jesus, the soldiers mocked and assaulted Him. They took off the purple robe and put His original garments on Him. They put on His battered and skinless shoulders the heavy cross, the cross of our transgressions, and in this state the soldiers made Him use whatever strength He had left to travel a gruelling trek, commonly known as the Via Dolorosa, uphill to a mountain called Golgotha. Tradition tells us that Jesus fell three times whilst carrying the cross and after the first fall, the soldiers, seeing that the Lord was struggling, and at the rate He was walking, may have died before He even made it onto the cross, so they lay hold of a man, Simon of Cyrene, a Gentile, and "compelled" him to bear the Lord's cross. Despite being hidden in an array of violent and inhumane acts, truly this was an amazing blessing for Simon to help carry the Lord's cross.

We too are called to carry the cross that has been put on our shoulders. In carrying our cross daily we are doing the will of God. We all have a cross to bear. Whether it is sickness of a family member or an ongoing family problem that seems to never go away, or the mere refusal of conforming to what some "friend" might push us to participate in unchristian behaviour, which at times seems like an impossible task. But remember, in each cross we have to bear, Christ is there carrying it with us. We are not in this problem alone but we have someone who can sympathise with the pain we are going through.

During Christ's journey down the Via Dolorosa, to Golgotha, "a great multitude of people followed Him," and many of the women "mourned and lamented Him." Yet Jesus, despite knowing His menacing fate, tender-heartedly gazes at them and tells them not to mourn for Him, but for the pains that will soon befall them and their children.

Jesus slowly and lethargically continues to carry His broken body as well as His heavy cross. The physical toll is unbearable, and Jesus again falls. It is here that tradition tells us a story. A young lady by the name of Veronica, seeing the Lord on the floor is touched with compassion, and without fear and in all boldness takes off the veil around her head and wipes the blood of the face of Jesus. The Lord was bleeding so severely that the veil was miraculously left with an imprint of Jesus' face.

The Lord's journey continues, and He has left a large trail of blood. His body is in distress, and His heart is broken, Golgotha is now in His sight. No words can describe the sheer carnage that His body is about to endure, and He knows it, yet He still soldiers on, to the fulfilment of our salvation, to do what He was born to do, to redeem the human race with His blood.

The Lord has reached Golgotha, and nothing else keeps Him moving toward His destruction except for the incredible love He has for you and me. St Augustine says that, "He loves each one of us, as if there were only one of us," meaning

What the Fathers Say

"Our Passover is Christ who has been sacrificed"

– Fr Bishoy Kamel

that He loves you as if you were the only person to ever live, as if He created the world for you and all His thoughts are always on you. So if He loves you as if you are the only one to ever live, then He also died for you as if you are the only one He was ever dying for. That's how much you mean to God! But why is it that when we are asked to show our love back, we don't? Jesus lived and died for you! Who are you living for? Who will you die for? We need to refocus our life on God. Just as we are the centrepiece of Christ's life so God needs to be the centrepiece of our lives. We were created by Him, for Him, and if we are not for Him then our existence has no purpose and our life has no meaning or depth.

Jesus is then shamefully stripped of His clothing and left naked. His cross is prepared and they throw the Master to the floor, and roll Him over as if He wasn't even human, until He is aligned onto the cross. The barbaric Roman soldiers then stretch out the Lord's body, and begin to drive

Reflections

If you were among the crowd that surrounded Jesus, would you have run away from the scene like the disciples or be forced to carry the cross like Simon or follow Christ all the way to the cross like St John and the women.

large blunted nails through His Almighty hands. Hands that lit up the sun, and moved the waters into life, are now being dulled and torn open, all for the great love He has for the creation that is tearing them.

All who are crucified have an inscription on their cross to indicate the reason they are being crucified. Pilate, in mocking the Jewish authorities as well as the Lord, writes "THIS IS JESUS THE KING OF THE JEWS." And with Jesus, they crucified two others who were both criminals.

Now once the soldiers had lifted the Lord up (as Jesus foretold) and set the cross in place, darkness filled the land, despite it being about midday. The soldiers then took Jesus' clothes and divided it amongst themselves. But when it came to His tunic, instead of tearing and dividing it, they cast lots to see who would now own it.

Throughout the agonizing event many, headed by the chief priests and elders, mocked and jeered and threw various heartless insults at the Lord. Some said, "He saved others; let Him

What the Fathers Say

"Have we realized what we do now? We are sprinkled with blood and the destroyer has no power over us at all."

- Fr Bishoy Kamel

save Himself if He is the Christ, the chosen of God." Others said, "Let Him come down from the cross, and we will believe Him." Many also who were passing by, "Blasphemed Him, wagging their heads." Even the two thieves who were crucified with Him, "reviled Him." Yet amidst all of these insults the Master and Lover of all looks up toward heaven and says, "Father, forgive them for they do not know what they do." The Master, whilst on the cross speaks seven sayings; the above is the first of these.

It is said that true love can soften the heart of even the hardest of criminals, and this is proven in the story of the right hand thief. One of the thieves, tradition tells us the one on the right, named Dimas, has a life changing experience in His encounter with the Messiah. Initially, this thief was among those who "reviled" the Lord, yet in seeing

People, Places and Things

Golgotha

Golgotha is the Hebrew name for the place where Jesus was crucified. It is known in Greek as Calvary, and is translated in English to mean "Place of the skull"

Simon of Cyrene

Cyrene is located in northern Africa, modern day Libya, and was under Roman rule. It is believed that Simon was a Greek speaking Jew from Cyrene who came to Jerusalem for the feast.
He is noted as being the father of Alexander and Rufus. Both sons are believed to have converted to Christianity.

The book of Romans, written by St Paul, greets a man named Rufus, and it is believed to be the same Rufus mentioned in the Gospel.

how He prayed for those who were mocking Him, and how Jesus loved those who were crucifying Him, and seeing how the creation had gone dark in revolt of the heinous acts committed against its Creator, he turned from the error of his ways and despite being nailed to a cross, began to follow Jesus.

The story goes that the left hand thief continued to mock Jesus throughout the crucifixion, and blasphemed and said, "If you are the Christ, save Yourself and us." But to Jesus' defence Dimas rebuked the other thief saying, "Do you not even fear God, seeing you are under the same condemnation? And we indeed justly, for we receive the due reward of our deeds; but this Man has done nothing wrong." Then humbly turning to Jesus asks Him, "Lord, remember me when You come into Your kingdom." Jesus touched by the repentance of His lost lamb replies, "Assuredly, I say to you, today you will be with Me in Paradise."

Reflections

Jesus forgave his enemies on the cross to teach us to forgive. Who in my life do I need to forgive?

How truly beautiful is the mercy and love of God, that with a simple apology and request of acceptance, He accepts a repentant blaspheming thief into His glorious kingdom.

WHICH THIEF?

Tradition tells us that Dimas was the right hand thief. The Gospels do not actually tell us his name or that it is the right hand thief who repents and is promised Paradise.

The 6th hour commemorates the Lord's crucifixion. From this hour onward, a lot more hymns are added.

The hymn "Tai shori", "This censor of pure gold..." is sung whilst the priest raises incense in all four directions, praying silent prayers for the people. This hymn is sung every regular Sunday, however, today it is chanted in the long sad tune. It is only sung this way, on this day, at this hour each year, and is one of the rare and most beautiful liturgical hymns in the Coptic Church.

Followed by "Tai shori" the congregation will chant the hymn of the cross, "Fai etaf enf", "He who lifted Himself up as an acceptable sacrifice..." this hymn is chanted 5 times throughout the year. Once for each of the two feasts of the cross, once in the 1st hour of Holy Thursday, once in the 6th hour of Good Friday, and the final time in the 9th hour of Good Friday.

The introduction, a section of, and the conclusion to the Pauline epistle are chanted, a hymn known as "Ti epistolee".

Then the "parts", which are usually read after the Gospel of the 6th hour in the Agpia, are prayed. However, they are chanted with a special sad tune.

Directly after this, the hymn "Omonogenees", "O Only Begotten Son..." is sung. This is another one of the rare and most beautiful hymns in the church. The words contain huge theological

and spiritual beauty. This hymn is only sung 2 other times, during the consecration of the Holy Mairoon/Chrism, and during the ordination of a bishop or patriarch. The long Trisagion hymn, "Agios" is then sung in its long mournful tune.

From this hour until the 9th hour, all the lights in the church are turned off as it says in the Gospel of Matthew 27:45, "Now from the sixth hour until the ninth hour there was darkness over all the land."

The hymn of the right hand thief is chanted. During this hour the right hand thief, Dimas, repented and asked for Jesus to remember him when He entered into His kingdom, and Jesus accepted his repentance. Therefore, the church sings the same words. "Remember me O Lord, O Holy, O Master, when You come into Your Kingdom.

After this hymn many churches will allow some time for individual prayer. Whilst prayers are being lifted up, deacons will sing from an incredibly moving selection of songs that relate to the Passion of our Lord, some even address the pain felt by His beloved mother, and the mother of us all, St Mary, as she stood at the foot of the cross gazing upon the mystery of her pain and salvation in the same scene.

Events

Friday
9ᵗʰ hour

Now, at the foot of the cross stood: Mary His mother, Mary His aunt, who was the mother of James and Joses, Salome who was the mother of James and John His disciples and also the wife of Zebedee, Mary Magdalene, and John the Beloved. The Lord looking down and seeing the pain in the eyes of His beloved who are present, is moved with compassion. Then looking intently at His most beloved mother the ever-virgin St Mary, and seeing the complete anguish that has filled her heart (St Mary knew the purpose of her Son's birth but nothing could prepare her for what she was witnessing), then looking at His beloved disciple, Jesus finds opportunity, even in His final and most traumatic and excruciating hours, to show love for those close to Him. To Mary He speaks, "Woman, behold your son!" then to John He speaks, "son, behold your mother!"

"And from that hour that disciple took her to his own home."

This is another beautiful scene amongst the horror of the crucifixion. The Lord, in all His pain and suffering, looked with compassion upon those who followed Him till the end. What is the extent of our following of God? How far are we willing to go for the One who loves us the most?

Then at about the ninth hour of the day, which is about 3 pm, Jesus cries out "Eloi, Eloi, lama sabachthani?" which translates to "My God, My God, why have You forsaken Me?" Many who were witnessing this, speculated and said that

He was crying out for Elijah to save Him, and mockingly cried out, "Let Him alone; let us see if Elijah will come to take Him down." Yet what they did not know was Christ was quoting a psalm by David the prophet, which if read in the context of the crucifixion, clearly points to Jesus as the Messiah. So Jesus, even at the point of death, is trying to save those who are present, and crying out for them to see that He is the one the prophets spoke of, He is Jesus the Christ, the Messiah of God prophesied of in Psalm 22.

Jesus, therefore feeling that it was approaching for Him to pass on, "knowing that all things were now accomplished," said, "I thirst!" Now one of the soldiers present spotted a vessel filled with sour wine, so he filled a sponge, put it on the end of a spikey stick like plant about 27 inches long known as a reed or a hyssop, and put it to Jesus' mouth for Him to drink.

Finally, with a cross drenched in red, with pools of blood seeping from the soon victorious cross, with a mangled body, neither covered by clothes nor by skin, Jesus cries out, "It is finished!" With His blood drained pale lips, He looks up to heaven, to His Father above and cries out, "Father, into Your hands I commit My Spirit!" Then bowing His own precious head, Jesus, of His own will, breathes His last.

Then the darkness was lifted from the land, and those who were in the tombs began to roam free, and the ground quaked, and the veil of the

What the Fathers Say

"Noah's ark is a figure of the church that was saved by the wood on which there hung the "Mediator between God and men, himself man, Jesus Christ." Even the very measurements of the ark are meant to point to the reality of the human body as He came as it was foretold He would come. As for the door in the side, that surely, symbolizes the open wound made by the spear in the side of the Crucified — the door by which those who come to Him enter in, in the sense that believers enter the church by means of sacraments that issued from that wound."

– St Augustine

temple dividing the Holy of Holies from the people was torn. And it being the Preparation Day, which is the day before the Sabbath, it was not fit for the bodies to remain on the crosses, thus to kill those being crucified more rapidly, they began to break their knees so that they may struggle more to lift themselves up to breathe. The legs of Dimas were broken, followed by those of the other thief, and finally they came to Jesus, but before they could break His legs, they found Him to be dead. To confirm whether or not He was still alive, they pierced His side with a spear, and "immediately blood and water" gushed out. At this final miraculous event, the centurion, whom tradition tells us was a man named Longinus, seeing what had happened, looks up and confesses, "Truly this Man was the Son of God!" Longinus later became a bishop and is mentioned in the Synaxarion.

People, Places and Things

Longinus

Commemorated on the 23rd of Abib / 29th of July. He was Greek by nationality, from one of the countries of Cappadocia. When Tiberius Caesar reigned, and appointed Pilate governor of the land of Judah, Longinus was one of the soldiers that accompanied him. When the time arrived that Our Lord wished to save the creation, Longinus was one of the soldiers that were in charge of crucifying the Lord of Glory. It happened that after the Lord had delivered up His soul, Longinus pierced His side with a spear, and blood and water flowed from His Side. Longinus marveled exceedingly when he saw this, and his amazement increased when he saw that the sun became dark, the curtain of the Temple was torn, the rocks were

Isn't this incredible! Longinus, a roman guard, a Greek by birth, a man who had been raised in pagan religions his entire life turns into a follower of a Man who just died on a cross, without even knowing what He was all about. The extent of the love and power of the crucified Christ was felt by Longinus, and in that moment He felt God pour His love upon him, and he turned and followed Christ. You never really know what something is made of until it is put under pressure, is squeezed and squashed, and when Jesus was squeezed on the cross He poured out an unlimited fountain of unconditional love, when He was dying on the cross He gushed forth a spring of life! Longinus later became a martyr for the sake of Christ.

What the Fathers Say

"A sign was written about the cross of Jesus, "Jesus of Nazareth, King of the Jews (INRI)" but a much more appropriate sign is one which reads, "The love and the sacrifice." "For God so loved the world that He gave His Only Begotten Son."

– H.H. Pope Shenouda III

split, and that the dead rose up from the tombs. He believed and realized all the miracles that Our Lord performed from His Birth to His Crucifixion. When the righteous Joseph took the body of the Savior, shrouded Him, and laid it in the sepulcher, this Saint was standing there with the guards when they sealed the tomb.

When Our Lord rose from the sealed tomb, Longinus was perplexed, and he asked God to explain to him this mystery. Our Lord sent to him the Apostle Peter, who told him everything that had been prophesied concerning the Redeemer. He believed, abandoned the military service, went back to his country, and preached the Name of Christ.

When Pilate heard about this, he wrote to Tiberius about him, who ordered his head cut off, and thus he received the crown of martyrdom.

Liturgical

At the start of the 9th hour the lights are switched back on, and the candles are re-lit.

Just as with the hymn "Tai shori" from the 6th hour, the hymn "Ti shori", "The golden censor is the virgin…" is sung whilst the priest raises incense in all four directions, praying silent prayers for the people. This hymn is usually sung every Sunday during a fasting season; however, today it is chanted in the long sad tune. It is only sung this way, on this day, at this hour each year, and is another one of the rare and most beautiful liturgical hymns in the Coptic Church.

Followed by "Tai shori" the congregation will again chant the hymn of the cross, "Fai etaf enf", "He who lifted Himself up as an acceptable sacrifice…" After which, another introduction, a section of, and the conclusion to the Pauline epistle are chanted in a hymn known as "Ethveti anastasis". Following, as in the 6th hour, is the "parts", which are usually read after the Gospel of the 9th hour in the Agpia. These "parts" are chanted with a special sad tune.

Reflections

When we are put under pressure what do we do? Get angry, use violence, swear or do we love as Christ did?

Events

Friday 11ᵗʰ hour

Now at the eleventh hour, about 5 pm, Joseph of Arimathea, a noble rich man, an influential member of the Sanhedrin, who did not condemn Christ but in fact was a follower of Jesus, but in secret, for fear of the Jews, requests of Pilate, that he may bury the Lord's body. Pilate surprised at the request, asks whether or not Jesus had really died so soon, and to his astonishment, He was confirmed to have died at the ninth hour, about 3 pm. Thus, Pilate allows Joseph to take and bury the Lord's body. So Joseph, together with Nicodemus, the Pharisee who originally visited Jesus at night in John chapter 3, went and bought one hundred pounds of myrrh and aloes; the amount used to bury a king. They also wrap His body in strips of linen. They then took the Lord's blessed body to a nearby garden, to a newly hewn tomb in which no one had ever been laid, and there they buried the Lord.

People, Places and Things

Joseph of Arimathea

Joseph was a rich member of the Jewish Sanhedrin, and was a colleague of those who tried Jesus illegally at night at the house of the high priest. He was noted for his righteousness and desire for God. Joseph was a secret follower of Jesus and is the one who asked for the Lord's body after His crucifixion, and placed the Lord in his own tomb. He was from a place called Arimathea, whilst the location is not known for sure; it is speculated

Even the earth gave Christ of its first fruits, "a newly hewn tomb in which no one had ever laid", God since the beginning asked for us to give Him the first of what we have, the best of what we have, and when we are ready, all of what we have with all our hearts too. The problem is, at times, we give so much to the world that we forget to give to the One that created it. God asked us for our first fruits, but most of the time we struggle to even give Him our third or fourth fruits. How can we not give back to the God that has given us all! That is robbery. And its not that God wants your first fruits in the form of money, He wants the first fruits of your time! He wants the first fruits of your heart! He wants you!

What the Fathers Say

"He is the One who, although He was silent in His passion, will not be silent finally in the day of reckoning. He is our God, even if unrecognised. He is already known among the faithful and all who believe. When He comes manifesting Himself in His Second Coming, He will not be silent. For although He was formerly hidden in humility, He will come manifested in power."

– St Cyprian

to be just northwest of Jerusalem.

Nicodemus

Nicodemus was a Pharisee at the time of Jesus who was a member of the Sanhedrin. He was noted as a teacher of Israel and a ruler of the Jews. Nicodemus first comes to Jesus at night for fear of his Jewish counterparts, which indicates rather cowardly qualities, yet by the end of his journey, he was bravely accompanying Joseph of Arimathea in burying the Lord's precious body.

PILATE VS HEROD

What the Fathers Say

"For the Lord died in those days, that we should no longer do the deeds of death. He gave His life, that we might preserve our own from the snares of the devil."

– St Athanasius

Luke 13:1 mentions an incident involving Pilate and the people of Galilee that seems to have caused hatred between Herod and Pilate. The verse says, "There were present at that season some who told Him about the Galileans whose blood Pilate had mingled with their sacrifices."

Pilate reigned at a time when various Roman governors around the world despised the Jews, and did what they could to provoke them. Pilate was not happy with how the Jews ran themselves and often tried to impose on this. Pilate, against all Jewish law, and in order to provoke the Jews, brought into Jerusalem Roman military crests with the image of Caesar.

Many Jews stood up to Pilate and refused to have this happen to their holy grounds, and it wasn't until Pilate saw that the Jews were willing to die rather than allow these crests into Jerusalem, that Pilate withdrew. What displeased Herod though was that Pilate put many armed undercover Roman soldiers on the streets of Galilee, which was Herod's diocese, and outside of Pilates's jurisdiction. These undercover soldiers shed much blood in Galilee and killed whoever deified either them, Pilate or Rome.

Liturgical

The priest opens the veil of the curtain and, with the deacons, ascends to the Sanctuary. This indicates that the heavenly is now connected with the earthly due to the death of Christ. "the veil of the temple was torn in two". The deacons who are wearing black or blue stole (budrashen) change them back to the usual red.

This hour begins normally, until we reach the prophecy of Jeremiah the prophet from the book of Lamentations. This prophecy contains very clear allusions to Jesus, and is sung with a beautiful tune that really moves the heart.

After the prophecies the deacons split in half, with one half moving into the inner Sanctuary and the other half staying outside. They then begin to chant "Thok te ti gom" for the last time antiphonically, with those inside responding to those outside. This "Thok te ti gom" is chanted with the playing of the cymbals and triangle, which previously was not played as it is not played during fasting or mournful seasons.

400 kerielaiyson's (Lord have mercy) are also chanted by the congregation. 100 Lord have mercy's in each direction of North, South, East, and West. These Lord have mercy's that are chanted are accompanied by prostrations. These are done that God may have mercy on all the earth and in all directions.

After the Lord have mercy's are chanted, the deacons begin the procession around the church and finish in the main sanctuary where the priest begins to bury an icon of Jesus in memory of the actual burial of Christ that occurred at that hour. While this burial is taking place the congregation chant the burial hymn called Golgotha. A very sad and mournful tune that evokes deep emotion in the hearts of the congregation that bring to mind the truth behind what is actually taking place.

The eldest priest will then begin to read the Psalms out loud, from Psalm 1 up until verse 5 of Psalm 3, "I lay down and slept". The congregation then continues the Psalms. These days, for the sake of time, this is done silently. The congregation will read all of the Psalms except Psalm 151, which is found in the Deuterocanonical books of the Bible. Psalm 151, as though it were some kind of continuation, is the opening hymn of the Apocalypse Saturday service.

What the Fathers Say

"Thus, my friends, today is a very great feast-day because the cross for Christians is not disgrace, but power."

- Fr Bishoy Kamel

Reflections

Do we go out of our way to do what is good and right, even if it means embarrassment and being an outcast, as was the case with Joseph of Arimathea and Nicodemus?

APOCALYPSE SATURDAY

Events

Apocalypse Saturday

It is the Sabbath, and the Jewish day of rest, thus all the people are not allowed to do any work, including the Lord's disciples. The 'Marys' and the women who followed Jesus were itching to go and anoint the body of Jesus, but could not. However, while they were worrying about anointing the Lord's body, something incredible was happening.

After His crucifixion, Christ conquered death and we say with the prophet Hosea and with St Paul, "Death is swallowed up in victory. O Death, where is your sting? O Hades, where is your victory?"

After the fall of Adam and Eve, God closed the gates of Paradise. To reopen them, the Lord had to be incarnate and become Man; He had to die and bridge the gap between heaven and earth. The moment Jesus died on the cross, having paid the price of our sins and having won salvation for us, Satan came to retrieve His soul, for at that time, when someone would die, they would descend to hades no matter how they lived their life. Thus, there were many righteous people who had descended to Hades. However, when Satan went to retrieve the soul of Jesus, he found that He was the Son of God and that he could not even approach the Lord. Satan found that Jesus had full power over His own life and could come and go as He pleased, and at that point Satan realised that God had defeated him, for Jesus truly was the Christ, the Son of God!

Hence the Lord, with full authority and all power, freed the souls of the righteous that were in Hades and thus conquered death, defeated Satan, and opened the gates of Paradise for those who love Him.

What the Fathers Say

"If He descends into hades, descend with Him. Learn to know the mysteries of Christ there also, what is the providential purpose of the twofold descent, to save all men absolutely by His manifestation, or there too, only them that believe."

– St Gregory of Nazianzen

Reflections

When it seems that Christ is not with me in tough times, be sure that he went to hades to bring the souls of those who believed in Him.

Liturgically speaking, this is a very strange yet beautiful day. Since Jesus died we are sad but because we remember that He will rise we are happy. Thus all the tunes on this day are partly sad and mournful and partly happy and joyous. After the burial on Good Friday while the curtains are closed the congregation begins to recite the psalms and stops at the final psalm without reading it. Thus the night of Joyous Saturday begins with the chanting of Psalm 151 as though we are continuing the service of Good Friday.

The night involves many liturgical activities including many readings of prayers recited by biblical figures such as Hannah the mother of Samuel and St Mary the Mother of God when the Lord was incarnate inside of her. There are many readings in the night that are only heard on this night that are very beautiful. The bulk of these

Hades

Hades, translated in Hebrew as Sheol as seen in many Old testament writings, is said to be the waiting place for the souls of those who are going to hell. However, before the birth, death and resurrection of Jesus, it was also the waiting place of all the righteous and just followers of God. While in the Old Testament, Hades or Sheol are used to represent the grave or the tomb, in the New Testament, it is used to represent a place of suffering and condemnation.

readings come from the Deuterocanonical books. These are books that are included in Orthodox bibles but are not counted in the more commonly printed other bibles. Beautiful stories such as Susana, Daniel and the idol, and many others that are all types of Christ, that is stories or historical figures that symbolize or remind us of things that Christ did, are included.

The night then goes on to the reading of the entire book of Revelation hence where we get the name "Apocalypse Saturday". Throughout this night the priest present is praying over oil that has seven lit cotton balls on top. At the conclusion of the reading of the book of Revelation the entire congregation is anointed with this oil.

What the Fathers Say

"Stretch your arms with Him and do not keep your feet from the nails. Taste with Him the bitterness of the gall. Rise early while it is still dark. Go to His tomb to see the glorious resurrection. Sit in the upper room and wait for His coming while the doors are closed. Open your ears to hear the words of peace from His mouth. Make haste and go to a lonely place. Bow your head to receive the last blessing before He ascends."

— St John of Dalyatha

ⲭⲣⲓⲥⲧⲟⲥ
ⲁ̅ⲛⲉⲥⲧⲏ

ⲁⲗⲏⲑⲟⲥ
ⲁ̅ⲛⲉⲥⲧⲏ

EASTER SUNDAY

Events

Easter Sunday

Now on the Sunday, on the third day after the Lord was crucified, on the first day of the week while it was still dark, and as the sun began to be seen, Mary Magdalene and the other women, went to the tomb of Jesus to complete the Jewish burial rights. As the women were discussing how they were going to roll open the large stone door of the tomb, "Behold, there was great earthquake" and an angel of the Lord, believed to be Archangel Michael, descended from heaven and rolled the stone door from the entrance of the tomb as a declaration of the resurrection of Christ, and sat on the stone. The angel's countenance was like "lightning, and his clothing as white as snow. And the guards shook for fear of him, and became like dead men."

The angel then looking at the women, said, "Do not be afraid, for I know that you seek Jesus who was crucified. He is not here; for He is risen, as He said. Come, see the place where the Lord lay. And go quickly and tell His disciples that He is risen from the dead, and indeed He is going before you into Galilee; there you will see Him." – Matt 28:5-7

The women were in shock, as we all would be. They did not know if they were asleep or awake, all that happened was too much for them to comprehend. Totally "perplexed" at what they just witnessed, they enter the tomb and find that the Lord's body was not there; the tomb was empty. All that was left were the tunics used to wrap the Lord's body. As the women increased in their confusion, two angels appeared to them in the tomb. They confirm what happened to the women saying, "Why do you seek the living among the dead? He is not here, but is risen!" The angels then remind the women of all that Jesus said concerning His betrayal, crucifixion and resurrection from the dead. Upon hearing the words of the angel, everything began to sink in. They remembered those things Jesus spoke while He was with them. So the women returned in fear and confusion at the words of the angel and told the eleven disciples all they had seen and heard. However, the disciples did not believe. Even the women themselves were not convinced, and "their words seemed to them idle tales, and they did not believe them." Thus the women "said nothing to anyone, for they were afraid." Afraid that perhaps they imagined the whole thing and were wishfully thinking all they saw.

But Mary Magdalene along with Peter and John went to the tomb and found it as the women had said. The body was gone and they saw the linen clothes lying where they were, as if the Lord had evaporated from them and the handkerchief that covered the Lord's head was folded and put in a separate place.

Peter and John then return home, marvelling at what they had just seen. But Mary Magdalene stayed at the tomb and began to weep, thinking she was losing her mind, that the angels were not real, and that someone had Jesus' body. Taking another look inside the tomb she found two angels, one at the foot of where the Lord's body was and the other at the head. They questioned her as to why she was weeping, to which she

What the Fathers Say

"Just as when He yielded up His spirit the earth shook, likewise in His resurrection He made the earth shake, so as to declare that He who died is the One to rise."

– Bishop Paul El Boshy

replied, "Because they have taken away my Lord, and I do not know where they have laid Him."

Mary then turns around to find Jesus standing behind her, but does not recognise Him, and thought that Jesus was the gardener. They then begin to converse:

Jesus: "Woman, why are you weeping? Whom are you seeking?"

Mary Magdalene: "Sir, if you have carried Him away, tell me where You have laid Him, and I will take Him away."

Jesus: "Mary!"

Mary Magdalene: "Rabonni!" (which is an affectionate way to say "teacher", or "my dear teacher")

Jesus: "Do not cling to Me, for I have not yet ascended to My father; but go to My brethren and say to them, 'I am ascending to My Father and Your Father, and to My God and Your God.'"

Then Mary returned to the disciples rejoicing and confirmed in faith and proclaimed to the disciples that the Lord had risen from the dead. Yet the disciples still did not believe.

What the Fathers Say

"The angels who conveyed the good news to the Bethlehem shepherds are now declaring His resurrection message. The Heavens and all its hosts declare Him. The higher spiritual hosts proclaim the Son, that He is God, even when in the body."

- St. Cyril the great

Then later that evening, Jesus appears to the disciples. He did not enter through the door, for it was locked, nor through a window, for they were all shut, yet He appeared to them and said "Peace be to you! As the Father has sent Me, I also send you." He then rebukes them for their lack of belief and blesses them, breathing in their faces and saying, "Receive the Holy Spirit. If you forgive the sins of any, they are forgiven them; if you retain the sins of any, they are retained."

What the Fathers Say

"You may say "how can I forgive what they did to me, it is enough for me to be silent and not answer evil for evil" no my brother this silence is not enough, in order to triumph from within, you have to forgive."

– H.H. Pope Shenouda III

Reflections

Jesus said: woman why are you weeping? There is nothing worth weeping about in this life because Christ is Risen.

The liturgy begins with the raising of incense. All tunes of this night are chanted in the festive joyful tune. In the raising of incense a hymn known as "the seven tunes" is chanted. This hymn is only sung on Easter, Christmas and the feast of Epiphany (the baptism of Christ). It is a tune that recounts all the seasons of the church and reminds us of the journey we have taken spiritually throughout the year.

The liturgy begins with the deacons and a procession of the oblations into the church and into the altar.

The liturgy of the word contains readings that are entirely focused on the Lords resurrection. Just after the reading of the Acts, the priest will close the curtains and begin to unwrap the icon that was symbolically buried in precious cloth, perfumes and flowers at the end of Good Friday,

People, Places and Things

Mary the mother of James and Joses and Mary the mother of Clopas.

Not much is known about these two, but we do know that they were brave followers of the Lord. They followed Him to the cross, and went to anoint His body after His burial, but instead were confronted with the Lord's mighty resurrection. It is believed that these two women may actually be the one in the same Mary. It is further believed that this Mary was the sister of the mother of God St Mary, since Mary the sister of the Mother of God married a man named Clopas in Greek but in Syriac is translated Alphaeus. Thus making James, James the Just

while antiphonally chanting a hymn with a deacon in the main chorus area outside the altar. The hymn that is chanted is derived from psalm 23 and is known as the resurrection re-enactment.

At the conclusion of the re-enactment the deacons will then parade around the church with icons and crosses of the risen Christ. The Gospel is then read and the liturgy of the faithful then begins. The Gregorian liturgy is usually prayed on feast days such as this.

What the Fathers Say

"Someone may ask "how can Christ be the first fruit of the resurrected while many rose before Him?" In fact there are some persons who rose from the dead before Christ but after their rising they died once more. Christ's resurrection was the one after which there was no death."

— H.H. Pope Shenouda III

or Less, who was the first bishop of Jerusalem, the cousin of Jesus.

Archangel Michael

Archangel Michael is said to be the chief of the heavenly hosts and is commemorated in the church on the 12th day of every Coptic month. He stood by God and fought for Him when satan rebelled against God. Archangel Michael is said to be the "trumpeter of the resurrection" and is said to be the angel that rolled away the stone of the tomb for Christ to walk through after His resurrection. He is also believed to be the angel that appeared to all that visited the tomb proclaiming to them the good news of the Lords resurrection.

The other Mary

Many believe that the other Mary is Mary the mother of God. In order to protect the virgin, the name of St Mary was not used. But all the believers knew that this name referred to Jesus' mother. The other Mary could also be a reference to the sister of St Mary the mother of God, who was also named Mary.

THE HANDKERCHIEF WAS FOLDED!!!

Notice that St John is clear in His Gospel about the location of the Lord's burial linen and handkerchief: "And he saw the linen cloths lying there, and the handkerchief that had been around His head, not lying with the linen cloths, but folded together in a place by itself." – John 20:7

It was common practise in Jewish culture that when one would leave the dinner table, they would either scrunch up their handkerchief and put it on the plate or with the other linen. However, if they were to return they would fold the handkerchief and leave it outside the plate. All that Christ ever did had a great symbolic meaning. This was a symbol of His return to earth, not only His return as the resurrected Messiah, but His glorious second coming on which He will ride on the clouds of heaven and draw to Himself those that pleased Him since the beginning.

Reflections

If you feel defeated by sin remember that Christ is Risen so that we may live a life of victory over sin and death.